Holistic Musical Thinking

Holistic Musical Thinking presents a comprehensive view of how people engage with music from a hands-on and heart-felt perspective. This approach embraces the teaching and learning processes as a multi-dimensional amalgamation of knowing, doing, and feeling through musical experiences. The result is a five-dimensional model that synthesizes cognitive, affective, and psychomotor learning with curricular integration.

With pedagogical applications, *Holistic Musical Thinking* offers a multi-faceted perspective that benefits both music teachers and their students. This innovative approach uses established research for a new model of musical thinking and taxonomy of musical engagement. Complete with classroom vignettes and pedagogical strategies, this book reframes musical thinking as a new direction in music education. Written for music teachers, teacher-educators, and their students, this book provides practical applications of the multi-dimensional Model of Holistic Musical Thinking for K-12 music education, and beyond.

Daniel C. Johnson is Professor of Music and Coordinator of Graduate and Undergraduate Music Education Studies at the University of North Carolina Wilmington, USA.

Routledge New Directions in Music Education Series

Series Editor: Clint Randles

The **Routledge New Directions in Music Education Series** consists of concise monographs that attempt to bring more of the wide world of music, education, and society into the discourse in music education.

A Different Paradigm in Music Education
Re-examining the Profession
David A. Williams

Eudaimonia
Perspectives for Music Learning
Edited by Gareth Dylan Smith and Marissa Silverman

Managing Stress in Music Education
Routes to Wellness and Vitality
H. Christian Bernhard II

Meanings of Music Participation
Scenarios from the United States
Edited by C. Victor Fung and Lisa J. Lehmberg

Flourishing in Music Education
Lessons from Positive Psychology
H. Christian Bernhard II

Holistic Musical Thinking
A Pedagogical Model for Hands-On and Heart-Felt Musical Engagement
Daniel C. Johnson

Holistic Musical Thinking

A Pedagogical Model for Hands-On
and Heart-Felt Musical Engagement

Daniel C. Johnson

Routledge
Taylor & Francis Group

NEW YORK AND LONDON

First published 2025
by Routledge
605 Third Avenue, New York, NY 10158

and by Routledge
4 Park Square, Milton Park, Abingdon, Oxon, OX14 4RN

Routledge is an imprint of the Taylor & Francis Group, an informa business

Library of Congress Cataloging-in-Publication Data
Names: Johnson, Daniel C. (Professor of music) author.
Title: Holistic musical thinking : a pedagogical model for hands-on and
heart-felt musical engagement / Daniel C. Johnson.
Description: New York, NY : Routledge, 2024. |
Series: Routledge new directions in music education |
Includes bibliographical references and index.
Identifiers: LCCN 2024016890 (print) | LCCN 2024016891 (ebook) |
ISBN 9780367220297 (hardback) | ISBN 9781032848587 (paperback) |
ISBN 9780429270383 (ebook)
Subjects: LCSH: Music–Instruction and study. |
Music–Instruction and study–Psychological aspects. | Holistic education.
Classification: LCC MT1.J62 H65 2024 (print) |
LCC MT1.J62 (ebook) | DDC 780.71–dc23/eng/20240419
LC record available at https://lccn.loc.gov/2024016890
LC ebook record available at https://lccn.loc.gov/2024016891

ISBN: 978-0-367-22029-7 (hbk)
ISBN: 978-1-032-84858-7 (pbk)
ISBN: 978-0-429-27038-3 (ebk)

DOI: 10.4324/9780429270383

Typeset in Times New Roman
by Newgen Publishing UK

Contents

Series Foreword

The *Routledge New Directions in Music Education Series* consists of concise monographs that attempt to bring more of the wide world of music, education, and society – and all of the conceptualizations and pragmatic implications that come with that world – into the discourse in music education. It is about discovering and uncovering big ideas for the profession, criticizing our long-held assumptions, suggesting new courses of action, and putting ideas into motion for the prosperity of future generations of music makers, teachers of music, researchers, scholars, and society.

Clint Randles, Series Editor

Acknowledgements

Thanks to the support and sharing of ideas with numerous colleagues, I have learned and grown through their collaborations to arrive at this point. The work of Timothy Brophy and Michael Palmer has been instrumental in developing ideas that served as a prelude to Holistic Musical Thinking and its theoretical framework. I would also like to acknowledge and thank numerous colleagues and friends for their encouragement and collaboration over the years. Those include my former mentors Robert Cutietta, Sandra Stauffer, Frank Abrahams, and many more. I would also like to thank Clint Randles as the editors at Routledge for supporting this project. I also acknowledge hundreds of students I have had the honor of teaching over the years. We have learned together about musical thinking, how to implement it in the classroom, and its importance to the profession. I also thank my supporters at the University of North Carolina Wilmington for a research reassignment semester when I developed and assembled the central ideas for this project. Most of all, I acknowledge JenneJ for her love, support, and graphic expertise throughout this journey.

More than a decade in the making, this book does not present new empirical or qualitative data. Instead, it is a synthesis of ideas from current and previous research that I have assembled into a new model that offers a multi-faceted perspective on musical thinking, specifically illuminating musical engagement and pedagogy. It provides research-based rationale for and application of Holistic Musical Thinking with implications for teaching and learning. My ultimate goal for the model and its application is to empower music teachers, teacher-educators, and their students to embrace and celebrate the many ways music is a complex and many-splendored experience.

1 Exploring Musical Thinking

Setting the Stage for Musical Thinking

Music, like love, is a many-splendored thing. This realization echoes the song lyrics from the 1955 movie of the same title and is the inspiration for this book. Informed by more than 30 years of experience as a music teacher and teacher-educator, Holistic Musical Thinking articulates observations I have made about the complexity of music teaching and learning. Convincing performances require a three-fold combination: understanding the musical background and conveying the emotional expression, as well as executing skillful technique. It is this three-fold knowing, feeling, and doing or holistic approach to music education that leads us to hands-on and heart-felt musical engagement. In noticing the intersection of multiple ways of knowing, I am fond of telling students, "We work in the *music* not the *technique* department!" Said another way, technique is a necessary but insufficient skill to deliver successful musical performances. The following chapters explain issues relevant to music teachers, teacher-educators, and their students so that they can thoughtfully explore the complexity of teaching and making music.

Recent and emergent research as well as historical sources provide both a firm foundation, rooted in tradition, as well as forward-thinking ideas from current scholars in the field. References from music and educational psychology summarize some of the main approaches in the field and their influence on contemporary music education. Although cognitive psychology has been a major focus in music education during the first two decades of the 21st century, this book goes further to address affective and psychomotor learning as key facets of music-making. It also reinforces emergent trends toward a broader,

DOI: 10.4324/9780429270383-1

holistic view of music education (e.g., Aróstegui et al., in press), and also provides a more specific focus on musical thinking in teaching and learning contexts.

Regardless of genre or style, people enjoy wonderful musical performances as moving, emotional, and memorable experiences. Our heads bob to the beat of rhythmic drumming, we sing along to soulful melodies, and we dance alone or with our friends as the music literally moves us (Smith, 2022). While music is remarkably entertaining and often impressive in this context, audiences often overlook the related thoughtful nature of music. Exploring how composers and arrangers "put it all together" requires a behind-the-scenes look at the creative processes involved. Therefore, we should consider music as a multi-modal and multi-dimensional experience – one which simultaneously engages us with the head, hands, and heart.

The central theme of this book, is a synthesis of well-established ideas into a new model of musical thinking. Like any model, it is a way of explaining, and understanding our experience. In this case, it embraces the multi-faced and multi-dimensional experience of music that touches us emotionally, moves us physically, and inspires our ideas.

By a holistic understanding of musical thinking, we mean a comprehensive view of the interconnected parts as a whole and complete experience (Merriam-Webster, 2024). As explored in this book, we can only truly understand and appreciate the whole musical experience by embracing its component processes – thoughtful, practical or praxial, and feelingful. Applying the axiom that "the whole is greater than the sum of its parts," we can appreciate musical experiences more fully and more completely when we examine the intellectual, physical, and emotional aspects of music. Similarly, one of the most meaningful aspects of music, its expressive qualities, are what scholar and music educator Steve Larson described as an "emergent property" which is a holistic attribute, greater than the components that interact to comprise it (2012, p. 18). To represent this approach, this book presents a five-dimensional, Model for Holistic Musical Thinking as the combination of cognitive, affective, and psychomotor, dimensions along with multipurpose ways to integrate other disciplines authentically and to engage learners creatively through guided musical experiences.

This book is for musicians, amateur and professional alike. Exploring musical thinking in a holistic way benefits professional musicians and their students as well as student-musicians and their teachers. Coming to appreciate music in a holistic way honors the thoughtful, practical, and ultimately feelingful work that combines to create musical experiences. Positive affective or emotional responses to music are the main attraction or source of enjoyment for listeners or performers alike (Juslin, 2016). Physical responses to music happen automatically (e.g., foot tapping and head nodding) and these actions relate to emotional reactions (Hodges, 2016).

By reframing music teaching and learning in terms that reflect the multi-dimensional and inherently meaningful nature of music, this approach represents a new direction in music education. It describes the creative and responsive processes that occur preceding, during, and following musical experiences. The resultant Model for Holistic Musical Thinking offers teachers and students a conceptual framework with practical applications. As discussed in Chapters 2 and 3, this text presents as an examination of established and emergent research on cognitive, affective, and psychomotor learning in combination with learning tools for interdisciplinary arts education and student engagement. By embracing musical thinking as an amalgamation of knowing, doing, and feeling, this Model for Holistic Musical Thinking articulates and enhances meaningful, multi-modal musical experiences with practical suggestions for memorable and effective music teaching and learning. Combining theory and practice of music education in this way extends established educational concepts, while also providing practical examples of the model in action in Chapter 4.

History and Theory of Musical Thinking

We begin our exploration of Holistic Musical Thinking with an orientation to learning and teaching music. These are deceivingly complicated enterprises. They comprise a three-fold, thoughtful, practical, and feelingful experience. On the surface, showing someone how to play or sing well is relatively simple. This is the main and most obvious part of all music teaching. Observing, imitating, and practicing musical skills are direct ways to replicate the teacher's performance. Below the surface, however, understanding, analyzing, and reflecting on musical experiences requires critical and creative thinking. On this deeper and more thoughtful level, engaging students in the process of transmission or sharing musical knowledge and skills is an age-old and continuing challenge for music educators. The practice of actually making music is central to its musical essence. Making and sharing music is key to both preserving musical traditions and to innovating new musical trajectories. Finally, communicating the story or message of any musical composition is perhaps the most long-lasting and touching part of any musical experience.

Created in 1965 by Richard Thomas, Comprehensive Musicianship through Performance (CMP) was an early example of holistic music teaching and learning. CMP offered a model for teaching performing with understanding in ensemble settings (Sindberg, 2009). As Thomas explained, learning music should focus on personal connections to music, thereby promoting self-expression as students discover musical meaning through performance (1970). This curricular reform showed the links between performance and making personal meaning by understanding musical context; this holistic approach clearly demonstrates cognitive, affective, and psychomotor learning. Perhaps the most important outcome of CMP was the term "comprehensive musicianship" which has entered the lexicon of music education in the decades that followed (Sindberg, 2009). As we will explore, a parallel Model for Holistic Musical Thinking expands on the premise articulated in CMP to broaden the student experience of music.

Definitions

Musical Thinking describes the range of cognitive, affective, and psychomotor processes that occur preceding, during, and following musical experiences. In more practical terms, we translate the musical ideas originating in our heads as we manipulate instruments with our hands or voices to create heart-felt musical experiences. For performers and listeners alike, these processes allow for meaningful, multi-modal engagement with musical experiences. While music teachers regularly explain musical concepts and ideas cognitively, the presence of music itself occupies another realm – that of the immediate experience. In that visceral and all-encompassing sense, "the exceptional power of music may be related to its ability to stimulate us aurally, visually, intellectually, emotionally, and physically, simultaneously" (Hallam et al., 2016, p. 905). Performing musicians, for example, regularly describe the experience of flow or making music in the moment (Nakamura & Csikszentmihalyi, 2020). This focused and immediate experience frequently combines thinking, doing, and feeling at various levels for musicking or live music-making (Small, 1998). As a counterpart, observers (other than those performing) describe music after-the-fact, frequently to understand music in terms of other contexts. Such descriptions integrate the essence or nature of musical experiences with other modes of understanding and expression. The Model for Holistic Musical Thinking presented in later chapters describes both the ways musicians engage with making music in the moment, and their extra-musical connections to other art forms and disciplines. This model encompasses how people intuitively make sense of musical experiences, whether as performers or observers, in cognitive, affective, and psychomotor terms.

Music is not a thing but an activity, something people do. Therefore, Christopher Small coined the term "musicking" in 1998 to highlight the importance of actively making and experiencing music in order to experience the power and relevance of musical engagement. Learning is a holistic process, experienced through authentic and multi-step tasks (Wiggins, 2015). Because both learning and music are holistic, best understood and experienced through multiple lenses or perspectives, an interpretation of musical thinking as holistic is a more accurate and authentic representation of this phenomenon.

Knowing About vs. Experiencing Music

Knowing *about* music and knowing music *through* musical experiences are distinctly different. Scholars such as Steve Larson have described this difference as *thinking in* and *thinking about* music with the main difference being present to the sound of music versus its abstractions (2012). In Western cultural traditions, knowledge about music typically comes in two forms – music theory and music history. Music theorists typically treat music as a puzzle, to be analyzed and dissected using musical elements. Music historians often treat music as examples of grand works, to be celebrated as marvelous achievements. Although explanations of music and musical events contribute to knowing about the historical and theoretical contexts, their importance is based on the experience of music itself. Both theoreticians and historians objectify music, treating it as something "out there" instead of and experience "in here" (Cook, 2021). In contrast, a more authentic approach to music education humanizes music as an embodied activity instead of a tangible product (Hodges, 2016; Lux et al., 2021; Smith, 2022).

With respect to music, learning about the discipline is not the same learning as doing discipline-specific activities. The difference lies in the level of authenticity and engagement. With active, engaged learning, students practice discipline-specific skills and develop corresponding tools to experience the work, in this case to make music (Ritchhart et al., 2011). By making music or musicking in this way (Small, 1998), learners engage in actual musical experiences, instead of reflecting on its related history, theory, or politics. A new direction along these lines incorporates both reflective and analytical thinking about the musical experience with the actual experience itself. Engagement with music in these multiple domains allows learners to uncover the most salient and personal musical meanings. By doing so, learners engage with the music learning experience to move toward to a personally meaningful and enduring relationship with it (Barrett, 2023; Barrett et al., 1997).

Pythagoras and other ancient Greeks articulated much of what we now know about the physical properties of sound and their relationships to the natural world. While our understanding of the physical properties of sound and silence are well-established, their meanings are not. How we make meaning from experiencing those acoustical phenomena is an ever-evolving pursuit. People interpret music based on their prior experiences. Therefore, teachers can expand learners' musical horizons and possibilities with exposure to novel musical traditions. They can also introduce students to cultures throughout the world because music is a ubiquitous component, found in every human society (Blacking, 1973; Mannes, 2009).

Historical Background

In the field of music education, musical thinking has a relatively brief but diverse history. In the 1960s, music educators focused on knowledge about and behaviors in musical contexts, with the intention of preparing students to become musically independent. By the 1980s, however, researchers and teachers found that students completed K-12 music education programs no better prepared to interact with music thoughtfully and independently than in the previous decades. As Eunice Boardman wrote in *Dimensions of Musical Thinking* (1989), the missing ingredient was students' ability to apply musical knowledge and skills to novel and unfamiliar musical situations.

In the decades that followed, researchers and pedagogues have used a range of educational psychology and general education research to develop approaches in an effort to provide this missing link. Some researchers have studied musical thinking in terms of composition and creative products (e.g., Hickey, 1997; Younker, 2000) while others have studied ways composers invent notation to encode their compositions (Barrett, 1997) and cognition in terms of neural networks (Fiske, 2004). Still others have framed musical thinking in terms of creative problem solving and cooperative learning (Wiggins, 2015). While these and other perspectives on musical thinking provided valuable insights into the cognitive and social aspects of musical experiences, they have not offered a comprehensive view of applied and affective modes of experiencing music. In contrast, a Model for Holistic Musical Thinking more completely embraces a wider range of multi-faceted, engaging, and meaningful music teaching and learning experiences.

Schools of Music

In contemporary pedagogy, the notion of *thinking* itself often conjures up images of traditional education and schools. While these institutions have an important role to play in establishing standards and organizing curricula, they do not circumscribe the extent of musical experiences. In other words, the version of music education offered by schools does not fully embrace the full range of musical experiences. Schools, and in particular American public schools, intend to benefit students and society at large by imparting musical knowledge and skills. Their purview, however, is not the limit of musical thinking. Instead, how people engage with music (each at their own level) is much broader and more authentic. Beyond concert halls and auditoria, the places and spaces for music education also include homes, churches, synagogues, garages, campfires, street-corners, and any number of other non-school, social gathering places.

Traditionally, music teachers focus on transmitting or passing down musical knowledge and skills to their students. Contemporary iterations of these skills include ear training, dictation, theoretical analysis, and music literacy. This transmission of skills constitutes training or drill and skill practice. With names such as Juilliard, Curtis, and Eastman, conservatories shape students for their future professional careers using an apprentice-master relationship (Kratus, 2007). This conservatory or apprenticeship model is common to both Western and, in a less formal sense, to non-Western cultures. In a perhaps dated view of this phenomenon, students are selected at a very young age and groomed for future training under the tutelage of masters who pass down centuries of knowledge and skills. In contemporary culture, however, new versions of this paradigm still persist (Kaschub & Smith, 2014). Elite institutions audition the most promising and accomplished students for professional training and specific career paths. While these world-class conservatories and universities promote high achievements for the selected few students, they also promote and perpetuate an exclusive view of musical participation. This paradigm applies to situations that highlight the talented few in not only classical but also popular musical genres. For example, contemporary television shows such as "American Idol" perpetuate the attitude that some people are more talented than others. The effect being to silence or subjugate others into quiet admiration of the idol's talent. The masses are idle while the talented are idolized (Johnson, 2013).

A contrasting view, less prevalent in Western societies and more common in African and other cultures, is that music is a natural and unrehearsed part of life. In this view, music is thoroughly and organically integrated into a range of other experiences. Music belongs to everyone because it is part of the universal human experience, as the cultural anthropologist John Blacking wrote in his seminal text *How Musical is Man?,* music is a universal feature of human cultures and societies worldwide (1973). This music-for-all paradigm honors all listeners' potential for musical thought. As Dewey wrote (1934), art is part of life and plays an integral role in a range of life experiences. He also advocated for play and discovery as natural means to developing understanding and personal growth.

A New Model

It is important to be clear about what the main educational aims are in music education. Some goals include developing musical independence while others emphasize performance skills and creative capacities. What kinds of related thinking are most musical, and how can teachers foster those thinking skills? Typically, *thinking* is termed a cognitive skill but thinking in fact closely relates to other psychological and physiological dimensions such as the affective and psychomotor, managing attitudes and motor skills. Successful musicians use all these together, combining them in ways to understand the composer's intent, then express those emotions through practiced performance. As a non-localized mental activity, music excites multiple regions of the brain, reaching well beyond the auditory cortex

(Hodges & Grun, 2018). Music is one experience that reaches multiple centers in the brain simultaneously. As the conductor George Szell said, "Music is indivisible. The dualism of feeling and thinking must be resolved to a state of unity in which one thinks with the heart and feels with the brain" (*Time Magazine,* February 22, 1963) (Letts, 2018, p. 287). For our purposes, we therefore define *thinking* broadly and holistically. The quality and category of thinking depends on both context and purpose, because it directly depends on the subject matter (Ritchhart et al., 2011). As such Holistic Musical Thinking provides musicians and educators with ways to understand musical ideas, make musical meaning, and feel their emotional effects simultaneously.

The model presented in this book provides ways to conceptualize and structure musical activities in terms of the many ways people experience music and to integrate those experiences with extra-musical connections. It offers a structured approach to musical thinking that parallels Copland's *What to Listen for in Music* (1963). In this often-cited text, he articulates three planes of music listening: the sensuous, the expressive, and the sheer musical. He organizes these planes in a hierarchy, from least to most sophisticated. While Copland's approach draws on years of experience as a composer, performer, and teacher, his focus is also largely cognitive – with the aim of facilitating more intelligent music listening. Comparatively, this holistic interpretation includes the cognitive aspects, while expanding to embrace the affective and psychomotor realms of experiencing music. This model values all three modes of musical experience equally – so that feeling and making music receive as much attention as thinking in and about music. The result is a more complete perspective on music as a universal human experience.

Music educators need a Model for Holistic Musical Thinking with applications to teaching and learning in order to articulate and scaffold related musical experiences in terms of the three traditional learning dimensions (i.e., cognitive, affective, and psychomotor). This is an important first step, "…to make the various forms, dimensions, and processes of thinking visible to ourselves" (Ritchhart et al., 2011, p. 5). The two teaching dimensions that complete the Model for Holistic Musical Thinking are curricular integration and musical engagement. Musical integration broadens and connects musical understanding to other subject areas. While forward-thinking musicians and teachers have at times recognized these important interdisciplinary connections, their work has not yet resulted in a cohesive taxonomy of musical engagement. This book presents such a model with the intention of exploring musical experiences through multiple dimensions from teaching and learning perspectives while also recognizing the transferrable thinking skills reaching across traditional disciplinary boundaries.

Thinking and Music

The term *thinking* implies cognition and an intellectual understanding of events or experiences. In this domain, the most important aspect of musical thinking is critical thinking. As a key 21st century skill, critical thinking is key to analyzing, synthesizing, and understanding musical elements (Trilling & Fadel, 2009). It also occupies one of the highest levels in Bloom's revised cognitive taxonomy (Anderson et al., 2001). An awareness of one's own thinking, or metacognition, is a related and essential first step to elevating the quality and efficacy of any thinking process. In musical terms, metacognition is a key factor in students' understanding their own musical potential and seeing themselves as creative musicians (Pogonowski, 1989).

Critical thinking in musical contexts enhances the definition of musical thinking. As advocated by Webster and Richardson, "music teachers must encourage children to think more deeply and more imaginatively about music and engage students…if real music learning is to occur" (1993, p. 7). Musical thinking, necessary for students to achieve musical independence (Boardman, 1989), is related to critical thought processes yet distinct from other forms of cognition. Webster and Richardson also suggested that musical thinking includes, "perceiving, representing, storing, and mentally manipulating musical sounds…sharing aspects of these musical sound structures with others in some form of product…and linking these musical sound structures with affect to achieve a deeper sense of personal meaning" (p. 8). Curriculum development in music education should therefore promote significant and meaningful music learning (Campbell & Scott-Kassner, 2019) including thoughts, ideas, and open-ended responses as well as vocabulary and activities. By augmenting students' awareness of music as a thoughtful experience, music educators can engage students more effectively, encourage them to think more musically, and inspire them to be more musically independent. All of these outcomes point toward one of the main goals in music education, musical engagement (Pitts, 2017).

Critical thinking in music also involves reflection, analysis, and evaluation in relation to musical activities with the purpose of developing one's own musical independence. Thinking is often understood as a mental process while feeling belongs to the sensory domain. In the arts, however, ideas are often the result of both thoughtful and feelingful experiences. In other words, feelings and thoughts are internal and interactive processes central to musical or other experiences (Tait & Haack, 1984). Furthermore, both affect and cognition play a part in higher-order thinking because thoughts are not emotion-free nor are emotions thoughtless (Dressel, 1988).

Woodford (2005) suggested that critical thinking encompasses elements of both generalizable and subject-specific approaches. Accordingly, in various musical settings, several researchers have promoted the value in students reflecting on their own thinking and encouraging them to use such higher-order thinking skills as hypothesizing, comparing, analyzing, evaluating, and creating (Kerchner, 2000). Applying these skills in different contexts is another example of an integrated approach. By taking advantage of generalizable cognitive skills, educators can enhance those skills and reach multiple content areas.

Previous investigations of critical thinking in musical contexts include problem solving, higher-order thinking skills, composition, music listening, and reflective thinking (Richardson & Whitaker, 1992; Younker, 2002). Other researchers have studied musical mapping, a technique common to many music series textbooks (Cassidy, 2001). This technique encourages students to think and rethink their musical perceptions, and to make meaning from music listening experiences, as documented through mapping activities (Blair, 2007). Musical mapping provides both kinesthetic and visual strategies to include feeling and knowing the musical experiences, furthering students' holistic understanding of the music.

Toward Musical Engagement

Although many textbook series and method books clearly outline curricula and activities for school music programs, they omit a crucial step toward realizing one of the main music education goals: facilitating students' growth toward independent musicianship (Wiggins, 2015). In other words, "unless we help students develop appropriate thinking processes--that is, learn how to think about music...the time spent in the music classroom has been essentially wasted" (Boardman, 1989, p. 2). More recently, music educators have begun to expand their focus beyond musical terms and general knowledge to include musical thinking and problem solving (Wiggins, 2002). These and other efforts have resulted in greater student engagement and overall musicality. As explored more fully in Chapter 3, a holistic approach to musical thinking moves beyond the cognitive dimension to more completely embrace the processes of teaching and learning music.

As explained in *Dimensions of Thinking* (Marzano et al., 1988) three types of knowledge are declarative, conditional, and procedural. Although not direct parallels, these three knowledge types match cognitive, affective, and psychomotor ways of knowing. In other words, "knowing what," "knowing why," and "knowing how," translate into musical contexts as, "what musical information," "for what emotional effect," and "how to produce or reproduce the sound?". While the term *musical thinking* implies an emphasis on cognitive skills, the act of making music or musicking (Small, 1998) most often requires psychomotor technique and also affords an affective response to be truly meaningful to the performer and the listener.

In addition to the cognitive dimension, emotional and physical understandings combine to frame a holistic approach to musical thinking and more completely describe the many ways people come to know and value musical experiences. Intellectualization of musical experiences results in cognitive distance from the experience of music. The disadvantage or deficit of that result removes the physical and emotional connection from the human experience. Music then becomes a mental exercise, devoid of meaning and life. Instead, teaching and learning music are purposeful activities and, as such as, should involve whole persons (Wells, 2000).

Reflecting on musical experiences and their meanings offers evidence anyone can use to validate their own musicality. This egalitarian and democratic view of musical thinking begins with the position that all people are innately musical. Further support for musical inclusivity comes from *The Music Instinct* (Mannes, 2009) which explores music holistically, as an innate human capability from an interdisciplinary perspective. As Evan Ziporyn wrote, "We are all musical thinkers, although we use a variety of mental tools to do the work" (cited in Bamberger, 2000, p. xi). By capitalizing on students' natural musical intuitions, educators can literally draw out their own musical potentials.

Societal Influences

Understood broadly, musical experiences relate to both politics and power. In educational settings, those dynamics come into play when teachers' power contrasts with that of their students. Lectures and other teacher-centered pedagogies are examples of this power dynamic. Associated with this relationship is the question of judging musical interpretations and improvisations. Although established musical traditions dictate the necessity of high-quality performance practices, informed teachers and empowered students ultimately *describe* rather than *judge* improvisations and musical creativity. Thoughtful educators can invite divergent thinking, a pillar of critical thinking, by asking: "What did you notice about that performance?" "What was the most valuable part?" "What do you wonder about it?" and other open-ended questions (Barnette, 2021).

In a mutually respectful and dialogic arrangement, both teacher and students have music to share. Taking a new direction in music education, holistic pedagogy that values and honors contributions from both teachers and students is open to discovery and divergent thinking. In this sense, music does not belong to teachers any more than to their students. The experience of making personally relevant meaning from sound and silence is equally available and valid to all people, regardless of their prior musical experience. The level of meaning-making may vary depending on the resources and comparative experiences each person has – the validity of the musical experience, however, is not dependent on their prior performance skills or theoretical knowledge. In other words, some of the best musicians are in kindergarten!

Holistic Musical Thinking aims to transform music education by eliminating the intra- and interdisciplinary divisions music educators and musicians in general often observe (Jorgensen, 2003). Instead, approaching musical thinking from a wide lens includes cognition, feelingful responses, and physical skills. As such, it validates an inclusive scope of musical practices and perspectives – applicable to both Western and non-Western traditions. This experiential and integrated model of musical thinking draws upon inclusive and holistic approaches to music education. Dating back over a century music educators have advocated for an inclusive approach. For example, Music Supervisors National Conference President Karl Gehrkens used the phrase, "Music for Every Child, Every Child for Music" at the 1923 annual meeting (Mark & Gary, 2007). Since then, the national music education organization has adapted this slogan in various ways to embrace all people's ability to think musically and to be musicians – each at their own level. This model of musical thinking favors the democratic and adaptable attitude as exemplified by active music-making pedagogies (e.g., Orff-Schulwerk, Kodály, Dalcroze, and Music Learning Theory). The effect is making musical experiences accessible through direct participation and first-hand engagement. In other words, instead of requiring music literacy as a pre-requisite, this avenue for music education is immediately access-ible to all participants. Through divergent thinking, this approach to musicking (Small, 1998) also fosters improvisation and creativity without specific, pre-determined performance results.

An AIT Conceptual Framework

The conceptual framework for Holistic Musical Thinking begins by understanding music on an elemental level – as a language of sound and silence. Its components are frequency, amplitude, and duration. In standard musical terms, those correspond to pitch, dynamic, and rhythm (Johnson, 2021). Music is a mental product, interpreted by people and based on prior experiences. Without that interpretation, the raw material of sound and silence means nothing. In other words, "music is what we make of it" (Ziporyn, cited in Bamberger, 2000, p. xi). In that sense, the analogy of music being a language is some-thing of a misnomer; because music has no absolute meaning, it is more esoteric and sophisticated in its communicative and expressive possibilities. More accurately, then, the perception of sounds and silence as musical events is the basis for musical thinking (Jarvis, 2005). Musical experiences depend on using aural perception to form thoughts about those sounds to develop disciplinary understandings of those experiences (Campbell & Scott-Kassner, 2019). Such an approach honors students as musicians and facilitates their musical growth through active involvement. Fundamental questions, then, are: what kinds of thinking are essential to that understanding? What kinds of emotions and attitudes might fit with those thoughts? What actions and skills are necessary to translate those ideas into musical realities?

Over the course of the past few decades, the scholarship on music teaching and learning has grown considerably. A number of new frameworks from the social sciences, particularly in education, psychology, sociology, and anthropology, have been adapted for music education, providing ways in which to interpret, organize, and conceptualize music teaching and learning in contemporary society. Some recent example publications include: *Culturally Responsive Teaching in Music Education* (Lind & McKoy, 2016), *Compassionate Music Teaching* (Hendricks, 2018), *The Oxford Handbook of Social Justice in Music Education* (Benedict et al., 2015), *Promising Practices in 21st Century Music Teacher Education* (Kaschub & Smith, 2014), and *Music and Music Education in People's Lives* (McPherson & Welch, 2018). These and other resources illustrate how making music is a political act (Cook, 2021).

Recent scholarly conferences have designated particular themes highlighting important foci for the field of music education. For example, the National Association for Music Education's "Music Research and Teacher Education Conference" (2018) focused on the importance of diversity, equity, access, and inclusion. The Suncoast Music Education Research Symposium highlighted "Learners Taking Charge" (2019), and the European Association for Music in Schools Regional Conference (2019) examined the topic "The School I'd Like," demonstrating more direct efforts to meet the contemporary needs of children and young people. The ultimate goal of each of these gatherings was to disseminate and share new findings, conceptualizations, and approaches describing how teachers and learners most effectively and meaningfully engage with music. These timely developments represent current thinking in the field of music education.

In addition to learning and understanding new frameworks and approaches, teachers need to determine which ones may be most useful and appropriate for their particular context. Keeping current with this expanding scholarship in music education is challenging, especially when considering the larger contexts of education and what constitutes meaningful engagement. To this end, we use an Authentic, Inclusive, and Transdisciplinary (AIT) conceptual framework as a way to understand and negotiate related aspects of music teaching and learning (Johnson & Palmer, 2019; Johnson, 2020). This meta-framework, based on recent and emerging scholarship, is the context for applying the Model for Holistic Musical Thinking. The result connects underlying AIT ideas with teaching and learning practices to benefit music teachers, teacher-educators, and their students.

Music is more diversified in its creation, production, performance, and use than ever before. Contemporary musical experiences occur in a variety of formats and contexts. There are traditional music experiences, such as performing in and listening to concert bands, orchestras, and choirs, and there are contemporary (technology-infused) experiences, such as playing in a rock band, composing music on a smartphone, performing music with others in a virtual setting, and spinning turntables at a dance party. Through these and other means, access to music creation is greater than at any other time in history. This technological revolution in our lives and its impact on music engagement is expanding the traditional notion of musicianship as well as the dynamic between teaching and learning (Fung, 2003). Kaschub and Smith noted that "performance-oriented musicianship... is shifting toward individual activity, or perhaps engagements that involve just a few people assembled in informal, social, and often digital contexts" (2014, p. 5).

Given this ever-evolving musical landscape, how are music educators acknowledging and incorporating these changes in practice? If a primary goal of music education is to prepare learners how to listen, connect, respond, perform, and create with these increasingly diverse and vibrant versions of music, perhaps music educators need a multi-faceted and holistic approach to teaching and learning music. Adopting the AIT framework provides a way to connect these ideas.

Authenticity

Authenticity, in the context of artistic activities, is a cultural construct that asserts the centrality of the individual's experience (Handler, 1986). This perspective supports the importance of artistic experiences as self-referential and internally valid. It also contextualizes creative experiences in the broader setting of established artistic practices. Therefore, authentic artistic experiences are those creative activities and products which the *individual* deems as valid within the context of what others understand and accept as a part of the larger art form. Even though *authenticity* itself is a subjective term (Gulikers et al., 2004), its importance in validating the individual's experience is paramount.

As one of the most important elements of credibility and validity, authenticity raises issues of relevance and agency from the learner's perspective. In formal or traditional school settings, the learner is often subject to the teacher's instructional decision-making. Those curricular decisions include choice of repertoire, interpretation, and procedures, just to name a few. In comparison to learners' informal or extra-curricular experiences, do these decisions support or limit their musical growth and development? In other words, how relevant and authentic is the curricular in-school learning to their extra-curricular musical experiences, values, and interests? Teachers' instructional decisions may have validity in terms of continuing established musical traditions, but those traditions may lack authenticity in terms of learners' lived experiences or to their inherent musical selves (O'Neill, 2018).

Another important realization from the learner's perspective is to recognize those students who do not participate in formal music education. Although many secondary school programs offer a range of ensembles with opportunities for student participation, a minority of the student body chooses to participate. For example, according to the 2019 summary report from the Arts Education Data Project, 91% of students in the United States have access to general or class-room music instruction through grade eight or age 14, but only 18% of students elect to participate in instrumental or choral music ensembles. Perhaps the in-school programs lack relevancy or authen-ticity for the majority of students. By reframing authentic music-making as relevant musical experiences, as defined by the learner, both formal and informal music teaching and learning can expand to include more numerous and more authentic musical traditions.

Both learners and teachers have insights and contributions to make to the teaching and learning process. From the teacher's per-spective, authenticity also has significance in terms of assessment in music education. An important and growing movement in music education focuses on assessment in praxial and philosophical terms (Brophy, 2019). The case for authentic assessment stems from a desire on the part of teacher-educators to have teachers enhance the ways they document and evaluate student work (Fautley & Colwell, 2018). By using a variety of field-based methods such as portfolios, exhibitions, performances, and demonstrations, teachers can enrich their assessment strategies to more authentically reflect the essence of musical activities (Darling-Hammond & Snyder, 2000).

A framework for authentic assessment includes five parameters: "(a) the assessment task, (b) the physical context, (c) the social context,

(d) the assessment result or form, and (e) the assessment criteria" (Gulikers et al., 2004, p. 70). These support applications to music teaching and learning because each of them relates to the ways musicians actually make music. More specifically, assessing musical tasks requires a musical purpose in an appropriate physical space/s with or for others to produce actual music with stated or understood criteria for success.

Applying the notion of authenticity to contemporary musicians has (at times) inspired students to "feel like real musicians!" The definition of "real musicians" lies in the authenticity of both the product and the process of making music (Johnson, 2013). Using 21st century technology, teachers can now separate performance technique from artistic engagement. By liberating the musician from hours of technical practicing, music technology can allow students to engage with and manipulate musical material virtually without first building the related performance technique. In this way, a much greater number of students and musicians can more freely and creatively make music, especially those without the traditional, technical background. This increase in accessibility raises questions of authenticity and validity. In other words, anyone who can work with computer software can create musical sounds…but is that "real music?"

Inclusivity

By its very nature, music is inclusive. In every culture throughout the world, people make and enjoy music (Blacking, 1973; Mannes, 2009). When we speak of inclusivity, we also acknowledge and celebrate diversity as an integral part of our world and our discipline. Diversity refers to people, places, cultures, perspectives, genres, as well as musical styles. If we wish to successfully open the world of music education up to all learners, we must connect with them. This may be in the form of culturally responsive teaching, in which we use cultural knowledge, prior experiences, frames of reference, and performance styles of ethnically diverse learners to make learning more relevant and effective (Lind & McKoy, 2016). It means adapting expectations or making accommodations so that learners with physical and emotional disabilities can have the opportunity for meaningful engagement with music and with others. It also means acknowledging and respecting individual identities. Ultimately, the connection we have with learners should be an informed and a compassionate one. As Hendricks (2018) explained,

> a compassionate music teacher in the 21st century is one who feels, understands, and even shares the students' enthusiasm for music and reaches out in ways that support the students' passions, visions, and desires – and then further awakens passion for music in their students.
>
> (p. 5)

By being inclusive, we avoid excluding or privileging specific perspectives, traditions, musical knowledge, and people, thereby creating space for more possibilities leading to the transformative nature of music in our lives.

The Oxford Handbook of Music Education and Social Justice (Benedict et al., 2015) is a prominent example of a timely and responsive publication that addresses representative topics such as democracy, racism, ableism, multiculturalism, and hegemony in relation to music education. Another recent resource articulating these important, interconnected, and inclusive themes is G. Preston Wilson's "Community of Practice and Social Justice" (2023) in which they describe the broad and meaningful involvement music can have in students' lives. For example, they articulate the understanding (cognitive), encountering (experiential), meaningful (constructivist), and doing (behavioral) aspects of learning through music. Similarly, contemporary social factors such as the Civil Rights movement influenced CMP, which led to multiculturalism and a more inclusive approach to music curricula (Mark & Gary, 2007).

Music education, especially at the secondary level, is most often focused on performing ensembles. Led by a conductor, this type of choral or instrumental ensemble depends upon the cooperation of many student-musicians to successfully perform arrangements and compositions on stage for an audience. Not only does this ensemble premise exclude many digital and electronic instruments, the repertoire choices often emphasize Western art music composed by white men. Ensemble directors often guide students in *re-creating* music of the past and present, instead of *creating* it in the present and for the future. A more inclusive mindset uses a democratic approach to curriculum and affords learners some level of autonomy (Philpott & Wright, 2018). In such inclusive classrooms, learners are empowered to express themselves musically, to develop critical thinking skills, and to contribute to the classroom culture.

Since the turn of the 21st century, national organizations and individuals alike have begun to question the lack of inclusion inherent in these ensemble assumptions and practices (Orzolek, 2021). Beyond more socially relevant and just repertoire choices, popular music ensembles (e.g., Modern Band), music technology classes, and music production studios now provide more opportunities for students to utilize digital technology for creating, performing, and engaging with music autonomously or collaboratively (Kladder, 2022). In the past, many of these opportunities existed in informal settings, outside of the classroom. Now, forward-thinking teachers are realizing the benefits of honoring and connecting to the students' musical lives and developing opportunities for sharing those in school (Tobias, 2015). Other examples of inclusive and diverse pedagogies include informal learning both in and outside formal school settings (e.g., Feichas, 2010). Inclusivity from these perspectives informs a holistic view of musical thinking by embracing a wide array of music-making possibilities, having the effect of increasing learner motivation and promoting lifelong musical engagement (Pitts, 2017). Ultimately a framework that is inclusive fosters more meaningful musical choices, connects both educators and students to contemporary society while amplifying the teaching and learning process. As Susan O'Neill wrote,

> we need to build on these shifts in thinking and continue to expand our awareness of the lens through which we view music learners in a digital age, examine more deeply and collaboratively the meaning and purpose of music learning, and develop music learning opportunities that promote connectivity across diverse perspectives, contexts, and cultural ecologies
>
> (2018, p. 164)

Toward that end, the Model for Holistic Musical Thinking is expansive and flexible enough to embrace the full array of music teaching and learning experiences. At the same time, it is structured and detailed enough to offer teachers and learners with meaningful directions to guide their musical journeys.

Transdisciplinarity

Before discussing the third theme of this framework, transdisciplinarity, we consider the ideas of multi-disciplinary or interdisciplinary studies. The similarities and differences among the terms inter-, multi-, and transdisciplinary are somewhat difficult to clarify and relate more to a mindset than a set of skills (Drake & Reid, 2021). Inter- and multi-disciplinary ideas or themes indicate a combination of two or more disciplines. That type of thinking or work often addresses the points of connection between or among different disciplines. Depending on the commonalities or differences among the disciplines, inter- or multi-disciplinary work can make important contributions that optimally strengthen the understanding or use of each distinct discipline.

Music, with its intrinsic connections to other disciplines, provides natural points of intersection and synergy in an integrated curriculum (Barrett, 2023; Barrett & Veblen, 2018; Harney, 2020). Music instruction that connects with standards from other disciplines features multimodal and interactive teaching presentations. The result is content-rich and standards-based instruction in both music and other subjects (National Coalition for Core Arts Standards, 2015). Outcomes of this approach highlight enhanced student understanding and engagement, including significant gains in achievement, attitudes, attendance, and behavior (Noblit et al., 2000, 2009). As such, integrated music education provides one of the most appropriate means of delivering collaborative and experiential activities, designed to engage learners and to deliver meaningful curricula effectively (Harney et al., 2024; Johnson et al., 2023).

Transdisciplinary work, on the other hand, involves creating new paradigms. This type of thinking opens new possibilities for scholars and practitioners who seek to move beyond inter- or multidisciplinary connections. Ideally, transdisciplinary vistas offer innovative approaches and blended lenses through which to view issues and develop new solutions. If music educators are to begin the Connecting process standard with meaningful and unified learning, a comprehensive, dynamic, and sophisticated approach is needed, i.e., transdisciplinarity. As Julia Marshall explained, "Transdisciplinarity…connotes a practice or domain that rises above disciplines and dissolves their boundaries to create a new social and cognitive space" (2014, p. 106). It is an interpretive lens that is globally open, acknowledging a new vision, yet remains grounded in lived experiences (Nicolescu, 1999).

  Transdisciplinary applications involve a unique set of cognitive skills for approaching problems which include perceiving, patterning, abstracting, embodied thinking, modeling, play, and synthesizing (Henriksen, 2018). Transdisciplinary experiences transcend divisions among the three traditional psychological dimensions of learning (i.e., cognitive, affective, and psychomotor). Transcending these divisions is necessary to reach an integrated understanding of the learning process (Visser, 1999). Transdisciplinary skills contribute to creativity and the capacities to envision and realize new experiences, new solutions, and new understandings. On a more practical level, it is important to remember that learning is a transdisciplinary concept. Applications of integrated music education within a transdisciplinary framework have also resulted in increased musical engagement (De Jong et al., 2021; Pike, 2016).

Summary

All people are musical thinkers, or at least they have the potential for musical thought based on the ways all people interpret sound and silence as "music" (Blacking, 1973; Mannes, 2009). By using musical elements and interdisciplinary connections as tools, they may enhance their musical thinking without losing ownership of their own insights and creativity. A Model for Holistic Musical Thinking articulates both teaching and learning processes through five dimensions within the AIT framework. The resulting model honors both the variety of musical experiences and diversity of avenues for music learning.

  Reflecting on musical experiences and their meanings offers evidence anyone can use to validate their own musicality. This egalitarian and democratic view of musical thinking begins with the position that all people are innately musical. It expands to develop students' musical potentials through continued engagement and interdisciplinary education. From a holistic perspective, those processes involve analytical, emotional, and physical engagement with music. To embrace the multi-dimensional and holistic nature of musical experiences, educators need to understand musical thinking and to make thinking musical. Beginning from the foundations of observation and exploration, teaching music has the potential to engage learners cognitively, affectively, and physically. With this opportunity, it is essential to be clear about what the main educational aims are in music education. Some goals include developing musical independence while others champion performance skills and creative capacities. In other words, music educators should ask themselves: what kinds of thinking are most musical and how can we foster those thinking skills?

Previewing acts to follow, we look ahead to the following chapters that comprise this book. Chapter 2 presents the background of these questions before presenting the Model for Holistic Musical Thinking in Chapter 3. Although there is no cogent answer about which kinds of thinking are the most musical, there are holistic ways to value and honor the multi-dimensional forms of musical thinking. More practically, multi-faceted instruction and interdisciplinary connections offer music teachers strategies to foster the most engaging forms of musical thinking. Chapter 3 presents the Model for Holistic Musical Thinking in terms of three learning and two pedagogical dimensions. They include a taxonomy for musical engagement and, taken together, allow us to realize musical thinking holistically. In Chapter 4, we examine the model in action by exploring exemplar lessons. Vignettes describe contrasting approaches to similar lessons through the lens of practical scenarios. The chapter concludes with suggestions for developing a musical thinking curriculum with implications for music teachers, teacher-educators, and their students.

References

Anderson, L. W., Krathwohl, D. R., Airasian, P. W., Cruikshank, K. A., Mayer, R. E., Pintrich, P. R., Raths, J., & Wittrock, M. C. (Eds.) (2001). *A taxonomy for learning, teaching, and assessing - A revision of Bloom's taxonomy of educational objectives.* Addison Wesley Longman, Inc.

Aróstegui, J. L., Christophersen, C., Nichols, J., & Matsunobu, K. (Eds.) (in press). *The Sage Handbook of School Music Education.* Sage.

Arts Education Data Project. (2019). *National Arts Education Summary Report.* https://artseddata.org/national_report_2019/ based learning across the curriculum. *Studies in Art Education, 55*(2), 104–127.

Bamberger, J. (2000). *Developing musical intuitions.* Oxford University Press.

Barnette, C. (2021). I notice – I wonder – I value. https://teachingwithorff.com/i-notice-i-wonder-i-value/

Barrett, J. R. (2023). *Seeking connections: An interdisciplinary perspective on music teaching and learning.* Oxford University Press.

Barrett, J. R., McCoy, C. W., & Veblen, K. K. (1997). *Sound ways of knowing: Music in the interdisciplinary curriculum.* Schirmer Books.

Barrett, J. R., & Veblen, K. K. (2018). Meaningful connections in a comprehensive approach to the music curriculum. In G. E. McPherson, & G. F. Welch (Eds.), *Music and music education in people's lives: An Oxford handbook of music education, Volume 2* (pp. 141–159). Oxford University Press.

Benedict, C., Schmidt, P., Spruce, G., & Woodford, P. (Eds.) (2015). *The Oxford handbook of social justice in music education.* Oxford University Press.

Blacking, J. (1973). *How musical is man?.* University of Washington Press.

Blair, D. V. (2007). Musical maps as narrative inquiry. *International Journal of Education & the Arts, 8.* www.ijea.org/v8n15/

Boardman, E. (Ed.). (1989). *Dimensions of musical thinking.* MENC - The National Association for Music Education.

Brophy, T. S. (Ed.). (2019). *The Oxford handbook of assessment policy and practice in music education.* Oxford University Press.

Campbell, P. S., & Scott-Kassner, C. (2019). *Music in childhood enhanced: From preschool through the elementary grades.* Cengage Learning.

Cassidy, J. W. (2001). Listening maps: Undergraduate students' ability to interpret various iconic representations. *Update: Applications of Research in Music Education, 19,* 15–19. doi:10.1177/87551233010190020104

Cook, N. (2021). *Music: A very short introduction* (2nd ed.). Oxford University Press.

Copland, A. (1963). *What to listen for in music.* McGraw-Hill.

Darling-Hammond, L., & Snyder, J. (2000). Authentic assessment of teaching in context. *Teaching and teacher education, 16* (5–6), 523–545.

De Jong, D. C., Pike, G., West, S., Valerius, H., Kay, A., & Ellis, S. (2021). Shared music, shared occupation: Embedding music as a socio-altruistic collective-and co-occupation in occupational therapy education. *Journal of Occupational Science, 28*(3), 374–387.

Dewey, J. (1934). *Art as experience.* G. P. Putnam's Sons.

Drake, S., & Reid, J. (2021). Thinking now: Transdisciplinary thinking as a disposition. *Academia Letters,* 1–6.

Dressel, J. H. (1988). Critical thinking and the perception of aesthetic form. *Language Arts, 65* (5), 567–572.

Fautley, M., & Colwell, R. (2018). Teaching, learning, and curriculum content. In G. E. McPherson, & G. F. Welch (Eds.), *Music and music education in people's lives: An Oxford handbook of music education, Volume 2* (pp. 257–276). Oxford University Press.

Feichas, H. (2010). Bridging the gap: Informal learning practices as a pedagogy of integration. *British Journal of Music Education, 27*(1), 47–58.

Fiske, H. E. (2004). *Connectionist models of musical thinking.* E. Mellen Press.

Fung, V. C. (2003). Possibilities for music education as a result of an expanded musicianship. In S. Leong (Ed.), *Musicianship in the 21st century: issues, trends and possibilities* (pp. 69–78). Australian Music Centre.

Gulikers, J. T., Bastiaens, T. J., & Kirschner, P. A. (2004). A five-dimensional framework for authentic assessment. *Educational technology research and development, 52*(3), 67.

Hallam, S., Cross, I., & Thaut, M. (2016). Where now? In S. Hallam, I. Cross, & M. Thaut. (Eds.), *The Oxford handbook of music psychology* (pp. 905–913). Oxford University Press.

Handler, R. (1986). Authenticity. *Anthropology today, 2*(1), 2–4.

Harney, K. (2020). *Integrating music across the elementary curriculum.* Oxford University Press.

Harney, K., Johnson, D. C., Languell, A., & Kanzler, C. (2024). Meaningful Music Integration: Disrupting K- 8 Classroom and Music Teacher Preparation and Practice. In M. Haning, J. A. Stevens, & B. N. Weidner (Eds.), *Points of Disruption in the Music Education Curriculum, Volume 2: Individual Changes.* Routledge.

Hendricks, K. (2018). *Compassionate music teaching: A framework for motivation and engagement in the 21st century.* Rowman & Littlefield.

Henriksen, D. (2018). *The 7 transdisciplinary cognitive skills for creative education.* Springer.

Hickey, M. (1997). Teaching ensembles to compose and improvise: Here are some practical ideas for incorporating the creative activities of composing and improvising into instrumental ensemble rehearsals. *Music Educators Journal, 83*(6), 17–21.

Hodges, D. A. (2016). Bodily responses to music. In S. Hallam, I. Cross, & M. Thaut. (Eds.), *The Oxford handbook of music psychology* (pp. 183–196). Oxford University Press.

Hodges, D. A., & Grun, W. (2018). Implications of neurosciences and brain research for music teaching and learning. In G. E. McPherson, & G. F. Welch (Eds.), *Music and music education in people's lives: An Oxford handbook of music education, Volume 1* (pp. 206–224). Oxford University Press.

Jarvis, S. (2005). Musical thinking: Hegel and the phenomenology of prosody. *Paragraph, 28*(2), 57–71.

Johnson, D. C. (2013, September). *Defining real musicians: How twenty-first century technology inspires musical creativity.* The Eighth Designs on eLearning International Conference: The Art of Disruptive Engagement, Wilmington, NC.

Johnson, D. C. (2020, January). *Frontiers in Authentic, Inclusive, and Transdisciplinary Music Education.* Lecture Presentation, Institute for Music Education, Ludwig Maximilian Universität, Munich, Germany.

Johnson, D. C. (2021). *Musical explorations: Fundamentals through experience.* Kendall Hunt Publishing.

Johnson, D. C., Harney, K., Languell-Pudelka, A. B., & Kanzler, C. (2023). Integrated arts education: perspectives and practices of teacher-educators and student-teachers. *The Teacher Educator*, 1–19. https://doi.org/10.1080/08878730.2023.2272182

Johnson, D. C., & Palmer, M. (2019, February). *Envisioning Contemporary Music Education through an Authentic, Inclusive, and Transdisciplinary Framework*. Research Presentation at the Twelfth Suncoast Music Education Research Symposium, Tampa, FL.

Jorgensen, E. R. (2003). *Transforming music education*. Indiana University Press.

Juslin, P. N. (2016). Emotional reactions to music. In S. Hallam, I. Cross, & M. Thaut (Eds.), *The Oxford handbook of music psychology* (pp. 197–213). Oxford University Press.

Kaschub, M., & Smith, J. (2014). Music teacher education in transition. In M. Kaschub & J. Smith (Eds.), *Promising practices in 21ˢᵗ century music teacher education* (pp. 3–23). Oxford.

Kerchner, J. L. (2000). Children's verbal, visual, and kinesthetic responses: Insight into their music listening experience. *Bulletin of the Council for Research in Music Education, 146,* 31–50.

Kladder, J. R. (Ed.). (2022). *Commercial and popular music in higher education: expanding notions of musicianship and pedagogy in contemporary education*. Taylor & Francis.

Kratus, J. (2007). Music education at the tipping point. *Music Educators Journal, 94*(2), 42–48.

Larson, S. (2012). *Musical forces: Motion, metaphor, and meaning in music.* Indiana University Press.

Letts, R. (2018). Emotion in music education. In G. E. McPherson, & G. F. Welch (Eds.), *Music and music education in people's lives: An Oxford handbook of music education, Volume 1* (pp. 285–291). Oxford University Press.

Lind, V. R., & McKoy, C. L. (2016). *Culturally responsive teaching in music education*. Routledge.

Lux, V., Non, A. L., Pexman, P. M., Stadler, W., Weber, L. A., & Krüger, M. (2021). A developmental framework for embodiment research: the next step toward integrating concepts and methods. *Frontiers in Systems Neuroscience, 15*, https://doi.org/10.3389/fnsys.2021.672740

Mannes, E. (2009). *The music instinct: Science & song*. PBS Distribution.

Mark, M., & Gary, C. L. (2007). *A history of American music education*. Rowman & Littlefield Education.

Marshall, J. (2014). Transdisciplinarity and art integration: Toward a new understanding of art-based learning across the curriculum. *Studies in Art Education, 55*(2), 104–127.

Marzano, R. J., Brandt, R. S., Hughes, C. S., Jones, B. F., Presseisen, B. Z., Rankin, S. C., & Suhor, C. (1988). *Dimensions of thinking: A framework for curriculum and instruction*. Association for Curriculum Supervision and Instruction.

McPherson, G. E., & Welch, G. F. (Eds.) (2018). *Music and music education in people's lives*. Oxford University Press.

Merriam-Webster (2024). *Dictionary*. www.merriam-webs ter.com/

Nakamura, J., & Csikszentmihalyi, M. (2020). The concept of flow. In C. R. Snyder, S. J. Lopez, L. M. Edwards, & S. C. Marques (Eds.) *Handbook of positive psychology* (pp. 279–296). Oxford University Press.

National Coalition for Core Arts Standards. (2015). *National Core Arts Standards.* State Education Agency Directors of Arts Education.

Nicolescu, B. (1999, April 19). *The transdisciplinary evolution of learning* [Conference presentation]. Annual Meeting of the American Educational Research Association, Montreal, Quebec, Canada.

Noblit, G., Corbett, D., & Wilson, B. (2000). *The arts and education reform: Lesson from a four-year evaluation of the A+ Schools program, 1995–1999.* The Thomas S. Kenan Institute for the Arts.

Noblit, G., Corbett, D., Wilson, B., & McKinney, M. (2009). *Creating and sustaining arts-based school reform: The A+ Schools Program.* Routledge.

O'Neill, S. A. (2018). Becoming a music learner: Toward a theory of trans-formative music engagement. In G. E. McPherson, & G. F. Welch (Eds.), *Music and music education in people's lives: An Oxford handbook of music education, Volume 1* (pp. 163–186). Oxford University Press.

Orzolek, D. C. (2021). Equity in music education: Programming and equity in ensembles: Students' perceptions. *Music Educators Journal, 107*(4), 42–44.

Philpott, C., & Wright, R. (2018). Teaching, learning, and curriculum content. In G. E. McPherson, & G. F. Welch (Eds.), *Music and music education in people's lives: An Oxford handbook of music education, Volume 2* (pp. 222–240). Oxford University Press.

Pike, G. O. (2016). *The past, present and future of music in educa-tion: A transdisciplinary framework designed to promote re-engagement and reform in music education for teachers, students, and the community* (Unpublished doctoral dissertation). Australian National University.

Pitts, S. E. (2017). What is music education for? Understanding and fostering routes into lifelong musical engagement. *Music Education Research, 19*(2), 160–168. https://doi.org/10.1080/14613808.2016.1166196

Pogonowski, L. (1989). Metacognition: A dimension of musical thinking. In E. Boardman (Ed.), *Dimensions of musical thinking* (pp. 9–20). MENC - The National Association for Music Education.

Richardson, C. P., & Whitaker, N. P. (1992). Critical thinking and music edu-cation. In R. Colwell (Ed.), *Handbook of research on music teaching and learning* (pp. 546–560). Schirmer Books.

Ritchhart, R., Church, M., & Morrison, K. (2011). Making thinking vis-ible: How to promote engagement, understanding, and independence for all learners. John Wiley & Sons.

Sindberg, L. (2009). The evolution of comprehensive musicianship through performance (CMP)—A model for teaching performing with understanding in the ensemble setting. *Contributions to Music Education 36*(1), 25–39.

Small, C. (1998). *Musicking: The meanings of performing and listening.* Wesleyan University Press.

Smith, G. D. (2022). *A Philosophy of Playing Drum Kit: Magical Nexus.* Cambridge University Press.

Tait, M., & Haack, P. (1984). *Principles and processes of music education.* Teachers College Press.

Thomas, R. B. (1970). Rethinking the curriculum. *Music Educators Journal, 56*(6), 68–70.

Tobias, E.S. (2015). Crossfading music education: Connections between secondary students' in and out-of-school music experience. *International Journal of Music Education, 33*(1), 18–35.

Trilling, B., & Fadel, C. (2009). *21st century skills: Learning for life in our times.* Wiley.

Visser, J. (1999, April 19–23). *Overcoming the underdevelopment of learning: A transdisciplinary view* [Conference presentation]. Annual Meeting of the American Educational Research Association, Montreal, Quebec, Canada.

Webster, P., & Richardson, C. P. (1993). Asking children to think about music. *Arts Education Policy Review, 94,* 7–11.

Wells, G. (2000). Dialogic inquiry in education: Building on the legacy of Vygotsky. In C. D. Lee & P. Smagorinsky (Eds.), *Vygotskian perspectives on literacy research: Constructing meaning through collaborative inquiry* (pp. 51–85). Cambridge University Press.

Wiggins, J. (2002). Teaching music through problem solving. In B. Hanley, & T. W. Goolsby (Eds.), *Musical understanding: Perspectives in theory and practice* (pp. 157–174). The Canadian Music Educators Association.

Wiggins, J. (2015). *Teaching for musical understanding.* Oxford University Press.

Wilson, G. P. (2023). Community of practice and social justice. In F. Abrahams (Ed.), *A music pedagogy for our time* (pp. 123–142). GIA Publications, Inc.

Woodford, P. (2005). *Democracy and music education.* Indiana University Press.

Younker, B. A. (2000). Composing with voice: Students' strategies, through processes, and reflections. In B. A. Roberts (Ed.), *The phenomenon of singing: Proceedings of the international symposium* (pp. 247–260). Memorial University.

Younker, B. A. (2002). Critical thinking. In R. Colwell, & C. Richardson (Eds.), *The new handbook of research on music teaching and learning* (pp. 162–170). Oxford University Press.

2 Domains of Teaching and Learning

Behind the Scenes

This chapter is an exploration of the learning and teaching domains that holistically inform the experiences of teaching and learning music. Organized into five dimensions, these elements combine to form a Model for Holistic Musical Thinking, representing a new direction in music education. Although used differently in some contexts, in this book the term "domain" refers to spheres of activity or knowledge while "dimensions" define and describe measurable aspects or features of those domains (Merriam-Webster, 2024). Before we explore this model more fully in Chapter 3, we begin by recognizing that the format for organizing the learning and teaching concepts in each domain is a taxonomy.

Taxonomies classify the components into an ordered or hierarchical system that indicates their relative relationships. The hierarchical levels of these taxonomies often serve as a measure of the level of thinking experiences that teachers plan for their students. As such, they are practical tools that educators use to develop educational objectives based on student readiness. Especially with respect to the learning dimensions, teachers work to engage their students in thinking at the highest level of the taxonomy as is developmentally appropriate while guiding their developing musicality.

Our discussion of learning taxonomies begins with the established dimensions that provide hierarchical structures to address learning as thinking, feeling, and doing. The first section of this chapter presents these taxonomies individually along with a preview of ways

DOI: 10.4324/9780429270383-2

they interconnect to inform music education practices (Johnson & Brophy, 2013). As explored more fully in Chapter 3, making direct connections among them allows us to formulate a more complete picture of musical thinking. The second section of this chapter presents taxonomies and models of teaching that focus on curriculum integration and learner engagement. The integrated or interdisciplinary aspect of music teaching is cross-curricular and embraces an array of concepts that music teachers can promote throughout the K-12 grade range. The notion of learner engagement describes the relative level of musical independence with attention to making music throughout the lifespan.

The Learning Domain

Learning is a complex task, and maximizing the thinking that learners do as they grow and develop poses a central challenge for educators. With an understanding that the underlying thinking behaviors are intrinsically developmental, educators seek to engage students sequentially with developmentally appropriate thinking exercises. While the developmental stages that students experience as they mature appear to be invariant, the types of thinking they demonstrate during learning activities are, by very their nature, hierarchical. As a support for maximizing students' learning potential, an enduring and primary goal for teachers is to develop thinking skills through an organized approach to learning. As the educational psychologist Jerome Bruner wrote in *The Culture of Education*, "One of the great triumphs of learning (and of teaching) is to get things organized in your head in a way that permits you to know more than you 'ought' to." (1997, p. 129).

   Discussions at the 1948 convention of the American Psychological Association (APA) focused on the low level of knowledge required on most university entrance examinations. In response, Benjamin Bloom and his colleagues began work to determine and classify the thinking behaviors that support learning. Their goal was to codify educational objectives to maximize learning and, in the process, classify the learning behaviors needed for success. Eventually, their work resulted in frameworks of three thinking dimensions: cognitive, affective, and psychomotor, each with a taxonomy of six, five, and seven levels, respectively. See Figure 2.1 for a radial display of the measurable levels of each as learning dimensions.

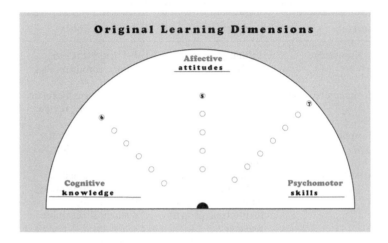

Figure 2.1 The Three Dimensions of Learning.

Cognitive Learning

In 1956, eight years after the APA convention, Bloom's work-group published their first handbook of educational objectives which focused on the cognitive dimension. Although *taxonomy* was somewhat unfamiliar at the time, they used the term, and this hierarchy of cognitive thinking skills is now known as "Bloom's Taxonomy." The six levels of this taxonomy are: knowledge, comprehension, application, analysis, synthesis, and evaluation. Organized from simple to complex, these levels have become a basic reference for teachers in all educational fields since their publication. Educators often place these levels into two meta-categories, indicating lower and higher-order thinking. The lower levels of the hierarchy being knowledge, comprehension, and application, while the higher levels are analysis, synthesis, and evaluation.

One important and foundational assumption is that each level of the taxonomy subsumes the skills mastered in the previous levels. In other words, as learners progress in complexity at each new level of the taxonomy, they are not only engaging the skills of the new level but also building upon the skills of the previous levels. For example, if students in a music classroom were at the Application level of thinking in a particular exercise, teachers assume that they have mastered the

Table 2.1 Summary of Bloom's Cognitive Taxonomy

Level	Description	Examples Actions
1. Knowledge	Recalling specific information, methods, or patterns	Label, list, memorize, name, reproduce, state
2. Comprehension	Understanding and using information	Describe, discuss, explain, report, restate, review, translate
3. Application	Using abstract concepts in specific and concrete situations	Demonstrate, illustrate, interpret, schedule, sketch, use
4. Analysis	Breaking down ideas or processes to understanding how their related parts fit together	Categorize, compare, contrast, differentiate, discriminate, distinguish, examine
5. Synthesis	Putting together ideas or processes to form a whole	Arrange, assemble, collect, compose, construct, create, formulate, organize
6. Evaluation	Making judgments about ideas and processes for related purposes	Appraise, assess, defend, estimate, rate, select, support, value

Source: Bloom (1956).

Knowledge and Comprehension levels of the exercise. Bloom also suggested verbs that operationalize the levels for classroom teachers to use when developing lesson objectives. See Table 2.1 for a summary of the cognitive taxonomy, descriptions of its six levels, and example actions.

In the decades since the publication of Bloom's first taxonomy, researchers and scholars have done further study about how learners develop and how thinking unfolds. Therefore, they proposed several interpretations, extensions, and explanations based on the original taxonomy. Most notably, educators revisited and revised the cognitive taxonomy in the 1990s to reflect new research data and to clarify the taxonomy itself (Anderson et al., 2001). Their revised taxonomy presented several significant improvements, with changes in terminology being the most obvious update to the original cognitive taxonomy. They shifted from nouns to verbs for each level in order to emphasize the procedural nature of the thinking taking place. This shift from concept to process

Table 2.2 Summary of the Revised Bloom's Cognitive Taxonomy

Level	Example Descriptors
1. Remembering	Retrieving, recognizing, and recalling relevant knowledge
2. Understanding	Constructing meaning through interpreting, classifying, summarizing, inferring, comparing, and explaining
3. Applying	Carrying out or using a procedure
4. Analyzing	Breaking material into parts and determining how they relate to one another
5. Evaluating	Making judgments based on criteria and standards
6. Creating	Putting elements together into a new pattern or structure

Source: Anderson et al. (2001).

Table 2.3 Summary of Knowledge Types in Bloom's Revised Taxonomy

Knowledge Type	Description
Factual	Knowledge of terminology and specific details
Conceptual	Knowledge of classifications and categories, principles and generalizations, theories, models, and structures
Procedural	Knowledge of subject-specific skills, techniques, and methods
Metacognitive	Knowledge about strategies, cognitive tasks, and contextual conditions

Source: Anderson et al. (2001).

is parallel to the current focus on artistic processes in the National Core Arts Standards [NCAS] (2015). The authors also renamed some of the levels: Knowledge, the lowest level of the original taxonomy, became Remembering; Comprehension became Understanding; Synthesis became Creating, which moved to the top of the new taxonomy; and Evaluation moved from its former place at the top of the hierarchy to the second highest level. Table 2.2 summarizes the Revised Cognitive Taxonomy, with an active verb as the name for each level and example descriptors that teachers can use to write learning objectives.

In the revised taxonomy, Knowledge is the foundation for the six cognitive processes. During their revisions, the authors also created a separate taxonomy of the types of knowledge used in cognition. These types are factual, conceptual, procedural, and meta-cognitive knowledge, as shown in Table 2.3.

In this hierarchy, we can see how cognition relates to other forms of knowledge. Its arrangement of ideas previews the relationship between the three dimensions of learning – cognitive, affective, and psychomotor. Applying these four levels of knowledge to musical contexts, Bennett Reimer (1992) suggested that knowing *within* (metacognitive) and knowing *how* (procedural) were supported by knowing *about* (factual) and knowing *why* (conceptual). Corresponding objectives for these knowledge types are, "to perceive, discriminate, feel, and evaluate works; to be aware of historical, social, cultural, political, and religious contexts, and to be cognizant of the issues that surround them, thus influencing perceiving, understanding, creating, and judging" (Fautley & Colwell, 2018, p. 271). This quote articulates the importance of connecting cognitive, affective, and psychomotor knowledge. It also previews our exploration of holistic musical thinking in terms of the relationship among these three knowledge dimensions.

Affective Learning

In the same sense that listening is more than hearing, music is more than sound (Johnson, 2020, 2021). In other words, music is the place where thinking and feeling meet (Sloboda, 2005). Many scholars and researchers have described this connection between music and emotions; one example is attributed to the Russian author Leo Tolstoy: "Music is the shorthand of emotion. Emotions which let themselves be described in words with such difficulty, are directly conveyed to man [sic] and music, and in that is its power and significance" (cited in Letts, 2018, p. 285).

To address these related emotional aspects of learning, Bloom and his contemporaries later focused on the affective dimension. Krathwohl, one of Bloom's colleagues, and his co-authors then published the second handbook, on the affective dimension of learning in 1973. This taxonomy presented a hierarchical view of attitudes and related affective components of learning including feelings, values, appreciation, enthusiasm, and motivations. Organized in five levels (i.e., receiving, responding, valuing, organization, and internalization), this hierarchy presented affective learning from the simplest to the most complex behaviors. See Table 2.4 for a summary with descriptors and examples that operationalize this dimension of learning.

Learning in the affective dimension is especially important in music and other performing arts because the feelingful impact or

Table 2.4 Summary of Krathwohl's Affective Taxonomy

Level	Description	Examples
1. Receiving	Awareness and passive attention	Describes, identifies, replies
2. Responding	Active participation, focused attention, and guided responses	Answers, practices, reports, selects, tells
3. Valuing	Acceptance and personal identification	Demonstrates, explains, identifies, joins, justifies
4. Organizing	Prioritizing, with a created value system	Defends, explains, relates
5. Internalizing	Characterization with persuasive, consistent, and predictable actions	Discriminates, performs, qualifies, verifies

Source: Krathwohl et al. (1973).

emotional effect of the arts together with the performance techniques involved are necessary partners to understand, express, and create. In one example from the Silver Burdett text *Music,* the authors explained that, "sometimes, when you listen, the music fills your thoughts and your feelings. That's the way composers and performers hope you will listen to their music, *musically*" [italics in original] (Crook et al., 1981, p. 108). In the decades since, music listening instruction has linked the cognitive dimension to the affective dimension and other forms of learning (Johnson, 2011). Related scholarship also supports the importance of feelings as emotions have an important and influential role in shaping musical thought (Thompson, 2015). Connecting this dimension with the other two forms of learning is an important advancement toward understanding musical thinking holistically, as we explore with a new model in Chapter 3. These ideas of feelingful engagement with artistic experiences factor prominently in a holistic view of music education and musical thinking.

Psychomotor Learning

The third dimension of learning identified by Bloom and his collaborators was the psychomotor dimension, even though they did not develop a psychomotor taxonomy. Instead, Harrow (1972) and Simpson (1972) authored two of the most well-known psychomotor

Table 2.5 Summary of Simpson's Psychomotor Taxonomy

Level	Description	Example Behaviors
1. Perception	Using to guide motor activity	Detects, differentiates, relates
2. Set	Dispositions or mindsets described by mental, physical, and emotional readiness to act	Begins, shows, volunteers
3. Guided Response	Imitation with trial and error, a beginning learning stage	Copies, follows, reacts, reproduces
4. Mechanism	Builds confidence and proficiency, an intermediate learning stage	Displays, manipulates, experiments
5. Complex Overt Response	Quick, accurate, and coordinated performance, a proficient learning stage	Builds, constructs, organizes
6. Adaptation	Modifies well-developed movement skills as needed	Alters, rearranges, reorganizes, revises
7. Origination	Creates new movement patterns with highly developed skills to solve problems	Combines, composes, creates, rearranges

Source: Simpson (1972).

taxonomies. Harrow used six levels to organize physical abilities as reflexive, fundamental, and skilled movements, which she linked to the learner's perception. More useful to most educators is Simpson's taxonomy which presented a hierarchical, developmental sequence of learning physical movement, coordination, and motor-skills. Requiring practice to develop, researchers measure these skills in terms of speed, precision, distance, procedures, or techniques in execution. There are seven major categories of behavior in this dimension, from simplest to most complex: perception, set (readiness to act), guided response, mechanism, complex overt response, adaptation, and origination. See Table 2.5 for a summary of this hierarchy.

Because music-making is an intensely physical task (Hodges & Grun, 2018), psychomotor learning is equally (if not more) important to music teaching and learning as compared to learning in the other dimensions. As we explore in Chapter 3, the relationship between music and motion is a direct and intimate one. As the scholar of music psychology Steve Larson wrote,

> our experience of physical motion shapes our experience of musical motion in specific and quantifiable ways – so that we not only speak about music as if it were shaped by musical analogs of physical gravity, magnetism, and inertia, but we also actually experience it in terms of "musical forces."
>
> (2012, p. 29)

In a related example, Frank Heuser highlighted actual music making as a quintessential context for music learning (2014). His contributions emphasize the importance of psychomotor or skill-based, musical understandings and foreshadow their implications for music-teacher preparation, with far-reaching implications.

All three traditional dimensions of learning (cognitive, affective, and psychomotor) factor into musical experiences. For example, understanding a sonata's historical origins and harmonic progression is important knowledge that informs a musician's approach to performing it on stage. Executing the requisite psychomotor skills with technical mastery allows the performance to be emotionally effective, moving an audience to joy or tears. Realizing this interconnectivity echoes comprehensive musicianship through performance introduced in Chapter 1. This curricular reform introduced decades ago by Richard Thomas (1970) is another example of connecting the learning dimensions to increase breadth and depth of musical engagement for more powerful learning experiences. Next, we explore two dimensions that define and describe the teaching domain: curriculum integration and musical engagement. These factors further assist educators in applying the three learning dimensions, as shown in the Model for Holistic Musical Thinking, presented in Chapter 3.

The Teaching Domain

Curriculum Integration

Music, with its intrinsic connections to other disciplines, provides natural points of intersection and synergy in an integrated curriculum (Barrett, 2023; Barrett & Veblen, 2018; Barrett et al., 1997). In addition, "musical meaning arises in part through such cross-domain mappings…" (Larson, 2012, p. 21). Specifically supported by the Connecting standard of the NCAS (National Coalition for Core Arts Standards, 2015), music instruction that integrates standards from other disciplines is known as Integrated Music Education (IME) and features multi-modal and interactive teaching presentations (Harney et al., 2024; Johnson et al., 2023). The result is content-rich and standards-based instruction in both music and other subjects. Outcomes of this approach highlight enhanced student understanding and engagement, including significant gains in achievement, attitudes, attendance, and behavior (Noblit et al., 2000, 2009). As such, IME provides one of the most effective means of delivering collaborative and experiential activities, designed to engage learners and to deliver meaningful and effective curricula.

Since the 1990s, innovative educators around the world have designed such curricula that integrate knowledge and activities from arts and non-arts subjects to address standards in those respective disciplines (Bresler, 1995; Cslovjecsek, 2010; Cslovjecsek & Zulauf, 2018). By using multi-modal and interactive teaching presentations, teachers focus on delivering standards-based instruction in both arts and non-arts subjects. Co-equal integration (Bresler, 1995) offers a curriculum centered on music as an equal partner with other subjects to achieve learning goals in both areas. Key to this curriculum are higher-order, transferrable thinking skills (Anderson et. al, 2001). This type of instruction results in significant learning gains among general classroom students as shown by written, aural, and kinesthetic outcomes (Johnson, 2011). As such, integrated arts education presents understanding, "on a totally different level of thinking – that is, as multilayered and symbiotic with other learning" (Russell & Zembylas, 2007, p. 288).

The most prominent benefits of integrated arts education for students are academic and social, with documented growth in both broad areas (Catterall et al., 2012; Goff & Ludwig, 2013; May & Robinson, 2016). More generally, arts integration fosters an increased appreciation for the relevance of the arts within the whole school curriculum (Anderson, 2014; Bresler, 1995; Hallmark, 2012; Wolf, 1992). As a parallel for teachers, the benefits are enhancing classroom learning environments (Cosenza, 2005; Deasy, 2008; Irwin et al., 2006), with greater academic achievement (Burton et al., 2000; Moss et al., 2018) and student creativity (Baer & Kaufman, 2012; Deasy, 2008; Root-Bernstein, 2001). Integrated arts instruction has also had the effect of increasing collaborative curricular planning (Barrett, 2023; Barrett &

Veblen, 2018; Barrett et al., 1997; Bresler, 2002; LaGarry & Richard, 2018; O'Keefe et al., 2016; Strand, 2006).

One classic approach to integrated arts education is Bresler's four levels of integrated instruction (1995). In order of increasing involvement, they are: subservient, affective, social, and co-equal. Subservient is the least involved type of integration and indicates that arts serve other disciplines (e.g., memorizing song lyrics to help remember a set of facts). A more integrated type of instruction is Affective integration, meaning that teachers use the arts to affect mood or inspire creativity (e.g., playing background music to help students relax or concentrate or drawing while listening to music). Social integration indicates that the arts serve a social function, such as musical presentations at school board meetings. The most involved type of integrated instruction is Co-equal, meaning that the teacher values and recognizes learning outcomes equally in both the arts and non-arts disciplines (e.g., exploring the concept of contrast in music and literature). See Table 2.6 for a summary of this approach.

Table 2.6 Summary of Bresler's Levels of Integration

Levels	Definitions	Examples
Subservient	Music serving other disciplines; trivial connections	Singing a song to memorize a set of facts; using music to "spice up" a lesson
Affective	Music enhancing a classroom atmosphere; music inspiring student creativity	Listening to background music to set a specific mood or promote concentration
Social	Using music to facilitate routines, manage student behaviors, or build a sense of community	Performing during the school's morning announcements; singing a song to promote proper handwashing
Co-Equal	A balanced partnership between music and another discipline, allowing students to simultaneously meet objectives and address standards in both areas	An in-depth exploration of a concept that music shares with another discipline, such as the concept of pattern in music and math or the concept of transformation in music and language arts

Source: Bresler (1995).

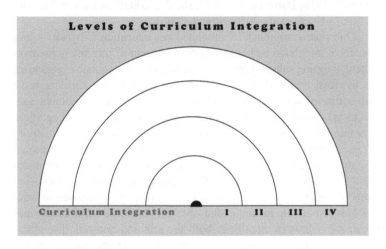

Figure 2.2 Levels of Curriculum Integration.

While Bresler's levels might appear to be listed in a ranked order, Hallmark (2012) argued against characterizing them as a "continuum that can suggest 'worst to best' teaching approaches" (p. 97). Following that reasoning, rather than labeling subservient, affective, social, and co-equal integration as inherently negative or positive, Bresler's levels may serve as descriptors of the various ways teachers incorporate music in classroom settings (Harney et al., 2024). Accordingly, subservient, affective, and social levels of integrated instruction all have educational value, e.g., singing songs to memorize content or enhancing a classroom community with collaborative music-making. At the same time, it is essential to recognize that simply promoting surface-level integration activities will not enhance the curriculum; an explicit emphasis on co-equal connections is necessary. See Figure 2.2.

Other approaches to differentiating levels of arts integration use three categories to distinguish the relationship between the art form and non-art form. For example, Barrett and her colleagues (1997) applied these ideas to specific disciplinary foci and used validity *within* the discipline, validity *for* the discipline, and validity *beyond* the discipline. Similarly, Snyder (1999) chose more active terminology to describe connections, correlations, and integration among disciplines.

In any system, the most important distinction to make is that not all "integration" is equal. What many educators term as integrated instruction is, in fact, only superficially related. Moving beyond such face validity is essential to harness the power and potential of inter-disciplinary learning. In one example of these possibilities, learners realize the intrinsic commonalities among disciplines to make their own connections for more meaningful learning. In other words, if teachers facilitate integrated learning, learners can participate in reorganizing, reconstructing, and transforming their own interdisciplinary understandings (Dewey, 1916/2018).

Descriptions of the most involved level of integrated arts instruction appear in several publications. Whether termed co-equal, integration with integrity, concept-based arts integration, two-way integration, or syntegration, forging this type of curricular connections is the most sophisticated and authentic (e.g., see Bresler, 1995; Snyder, 1999; Wolkowicz, 2017; Barry, 2008; and Russell-Bowie, 2009, respectively). Changing Education through the Arts (CETA), a professional development program sponsored by the Kennedy Center, promotes a similar co-equal version of arts integration. CETA defines arts integration as "an approach to teaching in which students construct and demonstrate understanding through an art form. Students engage in a creative process which connects an art form and another subject area and meets evolving objectives in both" (Silverstein & Layne, 2010, para 1). In each of these situations, the intention is to enhance students' conceptual understanding in one discipline through correlated activities in another.

More specifically, music instruction integrated with other subject areas is limited and sometimes of low quality (Abril & Gault, 2006; Bresler, 2002; Giles & Frego, 2004; National Center for Education Statistics, 2012; O'Keefe et al., 2016; Saunders & Baker, 1991). In other words, "a gulf exists between the idea of high-quality arts integration and its actual practice in schools" (Hallmark, 2012, p. 95). Accordingly, the majority of arts integration activities occurring in schools align with Bresler's subservient integration level, while those on the co-equal level are the most rare (Bresler, 1995, 2002; Wiggins, 2001).

Missing components for successful music integration include sufficient integration training for arts specialists (Hallmark, 2012), necessary administrator support (May & Robinson, 2016), and adequate planning time (Cosenza, 2005; Hallmark, 2012; LaGarry & Richard, 2018; May & Robinson, 2016; O'Keefe et al., 2016). As Hallmark wrote, "given traditional expectations of content sequencing, public performances or exhibits, and responsibilities toward large numbers of students, arts teachers rarely have time for quality arts integration work" (p. 93). Additionally, researchers have reported the need for increased collaboration among teachers (Bresler, 2002; Della Pietra, 2010; Munroe, 2015; O'Keefe et al., 2016; Strand, 2006) and effective arts integration professional development opportunities (Burnaford et al., 2013; Krakaur, 2017; LaGarry & Richard, 2018).

Considering this teaching dimension more broadly, connecting all the arts with non-arts subjects offers additional cross-curricular benefits that promote the inherent value of arts education in schools. As Hallmark asked, "Why should we assume that unintegrated, discipline-specific teaching is the best way to teach the arts in public schools?" (2012, p. 94). This provocative question highlights the assumption many teachers make about subject-specificity in classroom education. Hallmark's question also echoes the need to critically examine curricular assumptions in order to make informed decisions and to ensure validity for all learners (Kliebard, 1989). Furthermore, integrated arts education offers enhanced benefits to "at risk" students and those from non-traditional backgrounds (Anderson, 2014; Catterall et al., 2012; Johnson & Howell, 2009; Moss et al., 2018). In that sense, integrating the arts with other subjects creatively and effectively is more inclusive of all learners.

Innovative educators have promoted many systems for an integrated curriculum. In one example, a Comprehensive Arts Education Plan (S.B., 2010) includes Arts Education (arts as core, academic subjects); Arts Integration (arts as a catalyst for learning across the curriculum); and Arts Exposure (exposure to arts experiences).

The first component, Arts Education, relates to the arts as a "core academic subject" and articulates the importance of school-based instruction to develop proficiency in the arts. Arts Education is a collective term referring to a comprehensive and sequential education in four separate and distinct disciplines: dance, music, theatre arts, and visual arts. Defined as "core" by the federal Every Student Succeeds Act (2015), arts education is part of the regular school day and taught by licensed arts educators using the corresponding course of study.

The second component, Arts Integration, refers to using the arts as a catalyst for learning across the curriculum and in all areas of learning. In addition to offering a rigorous course of study in their distinct disciplines (dance, music, theatre arts, and visual arts), the arts are powerful tools for learning throughout the curriculum. When teachers create curricula that successfully integrate arts content and concepts with that from other subject areas, students are fully engaged in a multi-sensory learning experience through the application of multiple intelligences (Johnson et al., 2023).

The third component relates to the importance of Arts Exposure in providing practical settings for students to experience the arts. Either as creators, participants, or audience members, students learn about themselves and the complex world around them. In-school programming by professional artists reinforces the arts curriculum, while showcasing career paths. Artists also provide an inspirational model of the discipline, skill, and perseverance required to achieve excellence. Off-site student visits to art museums, theaters, or other arts venues demonstrate that the world beyond school grounds provides countless opportunities for discovery and active learning. Furthermore, it encourages students to become life-long learners and to engage with their communities. The interface between the arts sector and a school is an essential component of a comprehensive arts education and sustains a community culture of well-rounded citizens who recognize and value creativity.

Educators with different backgrounds intersect in a partnership to benefit students; certified arts and non-arts educators collaborate to provide standards-based curriculum; supplemental arts instructors support the arts standards and provide arts experiences that reinforce non-arts curriculum. At the nexus of these three, the collaboration constitutes sequential, standards-based instruction enhanced by focused arts experiences, with links between the arts and non-arts subjects (Richerme et al., 2012). All these ideas reinforce the ideal NCAS curriculum (2015). In particular, the connecting process addresses curriculum integration. Considering music specifically, IME offers novel and engaging ways for teachers to enhance their teaching effectiveness for multiple disciplines along with critical and higher-order thinking skills (Johnson et al., 2023). In addition, this contemporary approach promotes other transferable 21st century skills such as collaboration, creativity, and communication for an even broader impact on student learning (Martin & Calvert, 2018; Trilling & Fadel, 2009).

Because music provides a powerful avenue to involve students in non-arts learning, to promote abstract reasoning, and to foster critical and creative thinking skills (Fowler, 2001; Smithrim & Upitis, 2005), integrating music education with the rest of the curriculum offers multiple benefits to both students and teachers. Such meaningful interdisciplinary connections are key to the success of an integrated curriculum. Unfortunately, music teacher preparation is often discipline-specific and music teacher-educators tend to focus more on musical depth than curricular breath (Barrett, 2016, 2023). Therefore, developing interdisciplinary music teaching, requires focused and effective professional development (Johnson et al., 2023). Those connections in turn depend on both depth of student understanding and experiences along with breadth of participation and musical repertoire (Barrett & Veblen, 2018). By teaching for connections, educators can avoid the superficiality that undermines the potential for meaningful interdisciplinary learning.

Learner Engagement

A final dimension to explore before assembling the complete Model for Holistic Musical Thinking is the notion of learner engagement. Engagement, by definition, is the level of involvement and commitment to any activity (Merriam-Webster, 2024). More specifically in educational settings, we mean the concentration, sustained on-task behaviors, and focus that learners demonstrate. By engaging in the learning process, participants move from external observers to involved creators of their own understandings. In music, this process allows learners to form their own musical identities after having undergone often tedious drill-and-skill practice routines. The latter practice, however, is not necessarily a prerequisite for the former goal. Instead, skillful lessons can efficiently equip non-sophisticated learners with sufficient knowledge while imparting the requisite knowledge for them to engage fully as creators of their own music.

Independent of the subject matter, this type of engagement is central and essential to effective instruction and leads to more successful educational outcomes (Halverson, & Graham, 2019). This pedagogical certainty underscores the importance of engaging students in their own learning. Because learners naturally exhibit more engagement when given more autonomy and control over their own learning, a more learner-centered learning experience is necessarily more engaging than teacher-centered instruction (Bartel, 2002; Wiggins, 2015).

The idea of learner engagement is also linked with new directions in music education pedagogy. One of the more progressive directions is improvised pedagogy which advances the notions of autonomy, agency, and shared ownership (Johansen et al., 2020). In particular, the increasing emphasis on high-stakes test scores and other cognitively based measures has undermined the quality of education in general while deemphasizing democratic control of education (Biesta, 2015). For music and music education, the lack of learner engagement most often means lack of participation. Especially in elective ensemble classes, disengaged learners leave the group or depend on the instructor for all musical decisions (Philpott & Wright, 2018).

Although objectively measuring student engagement is a challenge, engaging learners leads to more successful instruction (Bulger et al., 2008). While this and other examples of research on student engagement uses electronic portfolios in computer-assisted environments (Barrett, 2007; Halverson & Graham, 2019), other researchers have explored engagement specifically in musical settings. For example, "Stages of Interaction with a Musical Work," in *Sound Ways of Knowing* (Barrett et al., 1997). See Table 2.7 for a summary of the

Table 2.7 Summary of "Stages of Interaction with a Musical Work"

Stage	Relationship	Learner Descriptions
0	None	disengaged from the musical instruction and is not at all attentive to the learning experience
1	Personal and incidental	recognizes some facets of the music and casual association
2	Personal and intentional	makes an effort to engage with the music as a learning activity, demonstrating more than a casual interest
3	Public	demonstrates an interest and preference for the musical activity to others, sharing positive responses about the music learning experience
4a	Performing	demonstrates skill in performing a musical work, an accomplishment as a result of attentive learning and focused effort
4b	Pedagogical	demonstrates skill as teachers, exhibiting ways learners transmit their musical knowledge to others
5	Long-lasting, personal, and professional	demonstrates an enduring shift in musical identity as the result of a memorable and transformative learning experience

Source: Barrett et al. (1997).

engagement stages with those relationships described in sequence from a lack of engagement to an enduring relationship with a work of art.

The intention or design of music-making experiences uses either a pedagogical or an artistic approach (Folkestad, 2006). In this pedagogical frame, the outcomes and purposes are explicitly teacher-defined and goal-oriented. By contrast, an artistic frame implicitly defines the value and purpose of the experience as the experience itself. While both frames promote learner engagement with music-making, the pedagogical frame lacks the autonomy and agency that the artistic frame provides. Perhaps the ideal learning environment has limited, teacher-defined learning goals in conjunction with rich, learner-centered activities to encourage musical improvisation and engagement.

Summary

Fundamentally, and perhaps organically, learners in musical settings integrate their thoughts, feelings, and actions. This holistic experience unites the way they understand, feel, and perform during a musical episode. In schooling, however, teachers tend to isolate or segment each of these aspects of the musical experience. Perhaps to organize their teaching approach, educators often disassociate these three aspects of music, although they synergistically make a complete musical whole. In fact, learners themselves come to study music as integrated and whole beings (Wells, 2000); honoring the thoughtful, feelingful, and skillful aspects of each student-musician is the most complete way for them to express each of those aspects in their own musicality.

This discussion of teaching and learning domains reveals that while music educators have been informed by and have engaged elements of existing taxonomies in their teaching, there remains a need for a taxonomy that informs music education and reflects the unique nature of thinking, feeling, and physically engaging in musical activities. Segmenting these dimensions has not allowed learners, teachers, or teacher-educators to understand their inter-connectivity or their interdependence. As discussed in the next chapter, recent practitioners and scholars such as Brophy, Shuler, and Hartenberger have made promising efforts to distinguish and organize unique components of musical thinking. What emerges as an advancement from their work is a Model for Holistic Musical Thinking, including a taxonomy for musical engagement, presented in Chapter 3. From both the learner and teacher perspectives, this new model combines all five dimensions to promote a more meaningful and complete concept of music teaching and learning.

References

Abril, C. R., & Gault, B. M. (2006). The state of music in the elementary school: The principal's perspective. *Journal of Research in Music Education, 54*(1), 6–20. https://doi.org/10.1177/002242940605400102

Anderson, A. (Ed.). (2014). *Arts integration and special education: An inclusive theory of action for student engagement.* Routledge.

Anderson, L. W., Krathwohl, D. R., Airasian, P. W., Cruikshank, K. A., Mayer, R. E., Pintrich, P. R., Raths, J., & Wittrock, M. C. (Eds.) (2001). *A taxonomy for learning, teaching, and assessing - A revision of Bloom's taxonomy of educational objectives.* Addison Wesley Longman, Inc.

Baer, J., & Kaufman, J. C. (2012). Divergent thinking. In J. Baer & J. C. Kaufman (Eds.), *Being creative inside and outside the classroom: How to boost your students' creativity - and your own* (pp. 13–60). Springer Science & Business Media.

Barrett, H. C. (2007). Researching electronic portfolios and learner engagement: The REFLECT initiative. *Journal of Adolescent & Adult Literacy, 50*(6), 436–449.

Barrett, J. R. (2016). Adopting an interdisciplinary approach to general music. In C. Abril & B. Gault (Eds.), *Teaching general music: Approaches, issues, and viewpoints* (pp. 168–182). Oxford University Press.

Barrett, J. R. (2023). *Seeking connections: An interdisciplinary perspective on music teaching and learning.* Oxford University Press.

Barrett, J. R., McCoy, C. W., & Veblen, K. K. (1997). *Sound ways of knowing: Music in the interdisciplinary curriculum.* Schirmer Books.

Barrett, J. R., & Veblen, K. K. (2018). Meaningful connections in a comprehensive approach to the music curriculum. In G. E. McPherson, & G. F. Welch (Eds.), *Music and music education in people's lives: An Oxford handbook of music education, Volume 2* (pp. 141–159). Oxford University Press.

Barry, N. H. (2008). The role of integrated curriculum in music teacher education. *Journal of Music Teacher Education, 18*(1), 28–38. https://doi.org/10.1177/1057083708323139

Bartel, L. (2002). Meaning and understanding in music. In B. Hanley, & T. W. Goolsby (Eds.), *Musical understanding: Perspectives in theory and practice* (pp. 51–70). The Canadian Music Educators Association.

Biesta, G. J. (2015). *Good education in an age of measurement: Ethics, politics, democracy.* Routledge.

Bloom, B. S. (1956). A taxonomy of educational objectives. Longmans.

Bresler, L. (1995). The subservient, co-equal, affective, and social integration styles and their implications for the arts. *Arts Education Policy Review, 96*(5), 31–37.

Bresler, L. (2002). Out of the trenches: The joys (and risks) of cross-disciplinary collaborations. *Bulletin of the Council for Research in Music Education, 152*(Spring), 17–39. www.jstor.org/stable/40319124

Brophy, T. S. (Ed.). (2019). *The Oxford handbook of assessment policy and practice in music education.* Oxford University Press.

Bruner, J. (1997). *The culture of education.* Harvard University Press.

Bulger, M. E., Mayer, R. E., Almeroth, K. C., & Blau, S. D. (2008). Measuring learner engagement in computer-equipped college classrooms. *Journal of Educational Multimedia and Hypermedia, 17*(2), 129–143.

Burnaford, G., Aprill, A., & Wiess, C. (2013). *Renaissance in the classroom: Arts integration and meaningful learning.* Lawrence Erlbaum.

Burton, J. M., Horowitz, R., & Abeles, H. (2000). Learning in and through the arts: The question of transfer. *Studies in Arts Education, 41*(3), 228–257.

Catterall, J. S., Dumais, S. A., & Hampden-Thompson, G. (2012). *The arts and achievement in at-risk youth: Findings from four longitudinal studies. Research Report #55.* National Endowment for the Arts.

Cosenza, G. (2005). Implications for music educators of an interdisciplinary curriculum. *International Journal of Education and the Arts, 6*(9), 1–7. www.ijea.org/v6n9/v6n9.pdf

Crook, E., Reimer, B., & Walker, D. S. (1981). *Silver Burdett Music.* Silver Burdett.

Cslovjecsek, M. (2010). How young children teach us to teach–Steps towards an integrative Music Education. *Hellenic Journal of Music, Education and Culture, 1*(1).

Cslovjecsek, M., & Zulauf, M. (2018). *Integrated music education: Challenges of teaching and teacher training.* Peter Lang.

Deasy, R. J. (2008). Why the arts deserve center stage. *School Administrator, 65*(3), 12–15, 17. www.aasa.org/SchoolAdministratorArticle.aspx?id=5962

Della Pietra, C. J. (2010). Preservice elementary classroom teachers' attitudes toward music in the school curriculum and teaching music. *Research and Issues in Music Education 8*(1), 1–15. https://files.eric.ed.gov/fulltext/EJ894769.pdf

Dewey, J. (1916/2018). *Democracy and education by John Dewey: With a critical introduction by Patricia H. Hinchey* (Vol. 1). Myers Education Press.

E. S. S. A. (2015). Every student succeeds act (ESSA). Public Law, 114–95.

Fautley, M., & Colwell, R. (2018). Teaching, learning, and curriculum content. In G. E. McPherson, & G. F. Welch (Eds.), *Music and music education in people's lives: An Oxford handbook of music education, Volume 2* (pp. 257–276). Oxford University Press.

Folkestad, G. (2006). Formal and informal learning situations or practices vs formal and informal ways of learning. *British Journal of Music Education, 23*(2), 135–145.

Fowler, C. B. (2001). *Strong arts, strong schools: The promising potential and shortsighted disregard of the arts in American schooling.* Oxford University Press.

Giles, A. M., & Frego, R. J. D. (2004). An inventory of music activities used by elementary classroom teachers: An exploratory study. *Update: Applications of Research in Music Education, 22*(2), 13–22. https://doi.org/10.1177/87551233040220020103

Goff, R., & Ludwig, M. (2013). *Teacher practice and student outcomes in arts-integrated learning settings: A review of literature.* Washington DC: American Institutes for Research.

Hallmark, E. F. (2012). Challenge: The arts as collaborative inquiry. *Arts Education Policy Review, 113*(3), 93–99. https://doi.org/10.1080/10632913.2012.687336

Halverson, L. R., & Graham, C. R. (2019). Learner Engagement in Blended Learning Environments: A Conceptual Framework. *Online Learning, 23*(2).

Harney, K., Johnson, D. C., Languell, A., & Kanzler, C. (2024). Meaningful Music Integration: Disrupting K- 8 Classroom and Music Teacher Preparation and Practice. In M. Haning, J. A. Stevens, & B. N. Weidner (Eds.), *Points of Disruption in the Music Education Curriculum, Volume 2: Individual Changes. Routledge.*

Harrow, A. (1972). A taxonomy of the psychomotor domain: A guide for developing behavioral objectives. David McKay.

Heuser, F. (2014). Juxtapositional pedagogy as an organizing principle in university music education programs. In M. Kaschub, & Smith, J. (Eds.), *Promising practices in 21st century music teacher education* (pp. 107–123). Oxford University Press.

Hodges, D. A., & Grun, W. (2018). Implications of neurosciences and brain research for music teaching and learning. In G. E. McPherson, & G. F. Welch (Eds.), *Music and music education in people's lives: An Oxford handbook of music education, Volume 1* (pp. 206–224). Oxford University Press.

Irwin, R. L., Gouzouasis, P., Leggo, C., & Springgay, S. (2006, March 6–9). *Investigating curriculum integration, the arts and diverse learning environments* [Paper presentation]. World Congress on Arts Education, Lisbon, PT. Retrieved from http://citeseerx.ist.psu.edu/viewdoc/download?doi=10.1.1.497.8270&rep=rep1&type=pdf

Johansen, G. G., Holdhus, K., Larsson, C., & MacGlone, U. (2020). Expanding the space for improvisation pedagogy in music: An introduction. In G. G. Johansen, K. Holdhus, C. Larsson, & U. MacGlone (Eds.), *Expanding the space for improvisation pedagogy in music* (pp. 1–14). Routledge.

Johnson, D. C. (2011). The effect of critical thinking instruction on verbal descriptions of music. *Journal of Research in Music Education, 59*(3), 257–272.

Johnson, D. C. (2020). The importance of listening in music education. In D. Worthington & G. Bodie (Eds.), *Handbook of Listening* (pp. 291–302). Wiley Blackwell.

Johnson, D. C. (2021). *Musical Explorations: Fundamentals Through Experience* (7th ed.). Kendall/Hunt.

Johnson, D. C., & Brophy, T. S. (2013). *Critical thinking in music education.* [Unpublished manuscript.]

Johnson, D. C., Harney, K., Languell-Pudelka, A. B., & Kanzler, C. (2023). Integrated arts education: perspectives and practices of teacher-educators and student-teachers. *The Teacher Educator*, 1–19. https://doi.org/10.1080/08878730.2023.2272182

Johnson, D. C., & Howell, G. (2009, September 10–12). *Drop-out prevention among at-risk students through integrated arts education: A school-university-community partnership* [Conference presentation]. Society for Music Teacher Education Symposium, Greensboro, NC.

Kliebard, H. M. (1989). Problems of definition in curriculum. *Journal of Curriculum and Supervision, 5*(1), 1–5.

Krakaur, K. (2017). *Arts integration for understanding: Deepening teacher practice in and through the arts* [Doctoral dissertation]. University of Maryland. Retrieved from https://drum.lib.umd.edu/handle/1903/19930

Krathwohl, D. R., Bloom, B. S., & Masia, B. B. (1973). *Taxonomy of educational objectives, the classification of educational goals. Handbook II: Affective domain.* David McKay Co., Inc.

LaGarry, A. E., & Richard, B. (2018). Arts integration in rural Minnesota: A collaborative arts integration framework. *Arts Education Policy Review, 119*(3), 146–157. https://doi.org/10.1080/10632913.2016.1236306

Larson, S. (2012). *Musical forces: Motion, metaphor, and meaning in music.* Indiana University Press.

Letts, R. (2018). Emotion in music education. In G. E. McPherson, & G. F. Welch (Eds.), *Music and music education in people's lives: An Oxford handbook of music education, Volume 1* (pp. 285–291). Oxford University Press.

Martin, B. H., & Calvert, A. (2018). Socially empowered learning in the classroom: Effects of arts integration and social enterprise in schools. *Journal of Teaching and Learning, 11*(2), 27–42.

May, B. N., & Robinson, N. R. (2016). Arts teachers' perceptions and attitudes on arts integration while participating in a statewide arts integration initiative. *Journal of Music Teacher Education, 25*(3), 12–26.

Merriam-Webster (2024). *Dictionary.* www.merriam-webs ter.com/

Moss, T. E., Benus, M. J., & Tucker, E. A. (2018). Impacting urban students' academic achievement and executive function through school-based arts integration programs. *SAGE Open,* 8(2), 1–10. https://doi.org/10.1177/2158244018773131

Munroe, A. (2015). Curriculum integration in the general music classroom. *General Music Today, 29*(1), 12–18. https://doi.org/10.1177/1048371315572878

National Center for Education Statistics [NCES]. (2012). Arts education in public elementary and secondary schools. U.S. Department of Education. https://nces.ed.gov/pubs2012/2012014rev.pdf

National Coalition for Core Arts Standards. (2015). *National Core Arts Standards.* State Education Agency Directors of Arts Education.

Noblit, G., Corbett, D., & Wilson, B. (2000). *The arts and education reform: Lesson from a four-year evaluation of the A+ Schools program, 1995–1999.* The Thomas S. Kenan Institute for the Arts.

Noblit, G., Corbett, D., Wilson, B., & McKinney, M. (2009). *Creating and sustaining arts-based school reform: The A+ Schools Program.* Routledge.

O'Keefe, K., Dearden, K. N., & West, R. (2016). A survey of the music integration practices of North Dakota elementary classroom teachers. *Update: Applications of Research in Music Education, 35*(1), 13–22. https://doi.org/10.1177/8755123315569739

Philpott, C., & Wright, R. (2018). Teaching, learning, and curriculum content. In G. E. McPherson, & G. F. Welch (Eds.), *Music and music education in people's lives: An Oxford handbook of music education, Volume 2* (pp. 222–240). Oxford University Press.

Reimer, B. (1992). What knowledge is of most worth in the arts? In B. Reimer, R. Smith, & K. Rehage (Eds.), *The arts, education, and aesthetic knowing: Ninety-first yearbook of the national society for the study of education* (pp. 20–50). National Society for the Study of Education.

Richerme, L. K., Shuler, S. C., McCaffrey, M., Hansen, D., & Tuttle, L. (2012). Roles of certified arts educators, certified non-arts educators, and providers of supplemental arts instruction. *SEADAE Arts Education,* 1–19.

Root-Bernstein, R. S. (2001). Music, creativity, and scientific thinking. *Leonardo, 34*(1), 63–68. https://doi.org/10.1162/002409401300052532

Russell, J., & Zembylas, M. (2007). Arts integration in the curriculum: A review of research and implications for teaching and learning. In L. Bresler (Ed.), *International handbook of research in arts education* (pp. 287–312). Springer.

Russell-Bowie, D. (2009). Syntegration or disintegration? Models of integrating the arts across the primary curriculum. *International Journal of Education in the Arts, 10*(28), 1–23. www.ijea.org/v10n28/

S.B. 66, Comprehensive Arts Education Plan, North Carolina General Assembly. (2010). Report to the Joint Legislative Education Oversight. https://webservices.ncleg.gov/ViewDocSiteFile/32811

Saunders, T. C., & Baker, D. S. (1991). In-service classroom teachers' perceptions of useful music skills and understandings. *Journal of Research in Music Education, 39*(3), 248–261. https://doi.org/10.2307/3344724

Silverstein, L., & Layne, S. (2010). *Defining arts integration.* Retrieved from www.kennedy-center.org/education/partners/defining_arts_integration.pdf

Simpson, E. J. (1972). *The classification of educational objectives in the psychomotor domain.* Gryphon House.

Sloboda, J. (2005). *Exploring the musical mind: Cognition, emotion, ability, function.* Oxford University Press.

Smithrim, K., & Upitis, R. (2005). Learning through the arts: Lessons of engagement. *Canadian Journal of Education/Revue Canadienne de l'Éducation, 28* (1/2), 109–127.

Snyder, S. (1999). Integrate with integrity: Music across the curriculum. *Journal for Learning through the Arts: Research Journal on Arts Integration in Schools and Communities, 1*(1), 74–89.

Strand, K. (2006). The heart and the journey: Case studies of collaboration for arts integrated curricula. *Arts Education Policy Review, 108*(1), 29–40. https://doi.org/10.3200/AEPR.108.1.29-40

Thomas, R. B. (1970). Rethinking the curriculum. *Music Educators Journal, 56*(6), 68–70.

Thompson, W. F. (2015). *Music, thought, and feeling: Understanding the psychology of music.* Oxford University Press.

Trilling, B., & Fadel, C. (2009). *21st century skills: Learning for life in our times.* John Wiley & Sons.

Wells, G. (2000). Dialogic inquiry in education: Building on the legacy of Vygotsky. In C. D. Lee & P. Smagorinsky (Eds.), *Vygotskian perspectives on literacy research: Constructing meaning through collaborative inquiry* (pp. 51–85). Cambridge University Press.

Wiggins, R. A. (2001). Interdisciplinary curriculum: Music educator concerns. *Music Educators Journal, 87*(5), 40–44. https://doi.org/10.2307/3399707

Wiggins, J. (2015). *Teaching for musical understanding.* Oxford University Press.

Wolf, D. P. (1992). Assessment as an episode of learning. *Assessment Update 4*(1), 5–14.

Wolkowicz, T. (2017). Concept-based arts integration: Lessons learned from an application in music and biology. *Music Educators Journal, 103*(4), 40–47. https://doi.org/10.1177/0027432117697004

3 A Pedagogical Model for Holistic Musical Thinking

Previous Ideas about Musical Thinking

In this chapter, we examine musical thinking in terms of three learning and two teaching dimensions. As described in Chapter 2, the learning dimensions are the cognitive, affective, and psychomotor processes, well-established in educational psychology (Hoque, 2016), while the two teaching dimensions are curriculum integration and musical engagement. These five parameters define a new Model for Holistic Musical Thinking that describes both teaching and learning processes to provide a more complete understanding than in separate taxonomies. As demonstrated in Chapter 4, this holistic view is also a practical tool for music teachers, teacher-educators, and their students when designing and reflecting on instruction. Before discussing specifics of the new model, we examine research on earlier concepts of musical thinking as critical thinking and related approaches (Johnson & Brophy, 2013).

Initial Developments

Musical thinking has taken the form of critical thinking within the general body of theory and knowledge pertaining to critical thinking across all subjects (Younker, 2002). By critical thinking, we mean the more advanced three levels of Bloom's Revised Cognitive Taxonomy: analyzing, evaluating, and creating (Anderson et al., 2001; Trilling & Fadel, 2009). This complex area of educational theory, philosophy, and practice has matured considerably since the turn of the century. Any discussion of critical thinking in music first becomes a task of defining what this term means in musical settings

DOI: 10.4324/9780429270383-3

and then how music educators can evaluate students' critical thinking processes (Richardson & Whitaker, 1992). Accordingly, we explore a model that leads readers toward answers for both questions: defining critical thinking in music, and developing strategies to assess students' musical thinking. The following discussion presents an overview of some of the work done to define and describe critical thinking in the arts and in music during the 1980s and 1990s, which laid the foundation for the development of taxonomic frameworks in the early 2000s.

Paulo Freire, in his seminal work *Pedagogy of the Oppressed* (1970/ 2000), framed critical theory as the combination of critical thinking, feeling, and action. Examining his writing, Cara Faith Bernard wrote that some teachers approach critical thinking as a procedure linked to measurable outcomes (2023). She asserted that critical thinking in music education is not limited to teacher-directed problem-solving but instead inclusive of, "deep thinking, feeling, and action" (p. 175). She also wrote,

> during a moment in education where instrumental, outcome based critical thinking, high stakes testing, and accountability drive instruction, music teachers must purposefully provide students opportunities to engage with perspectives and ideas that challenge and invite them to take part in their learning in ways where they might see themselves as active curators of knowledge and experience.
>
> (p. 195)

In these terms, we understand the holistic nature of critical thinking to include the emotional and active realms.

Our discussion of musical thinking begins with an important publication on the nature of thinking in general. Written by Robert Marzano and his colleagues, *Dimensions of Thinking* (1988) outlined five dimensions that apply broadly to thinking skills in educational settings: metacognition, critical and creative thinking, thinking processes, core thinking skills, and the influence of content-area knowledge on thinking skills. To apply the content-area dimension to music, a group of authors led by Eunice Boardman published *Dimensions of Musical Thinking* in 1989. In this book, they explored definitions of thinking with implications for musicians, and applications in a range of musical contexts. As Boardman explained, this text articulated four perspectives on content knowledge, intended to move students beyond knowledge and behavior toward musical independence. Those perspectives interpreted musical content knowledge as special approaches to investigating musical problems, organized into schemas or packages of related knowledge, as a model or metaphor for emotional self-expression, and shaped by shifts from behavioral to cognitive psychology in music.

Researchers have constructed the taxonomies of the cognitive, affective, and psychomotor dimensions to assist general education teachers in to operationalize thinking and write educational objectives. Similarly, conceptions and taxonomies of musical thinking and processing have developed as a means to describe these processes for music teachers. As explained in the following sections, researchers and scholars based their early conceptions of musical thinking on an array of separate approaches to critical thinking, feeling, and doing.

Both the *Dimensions of Thinking* (Marzano et al., 1988) and *Dimensions of Musical Thinking* (Boardman, 1989) were part of a concerted effort by the profession to understand and define critical thinking across content areas. While none of the authors in Boardman's edited 1989 volume presented a taxonomy of thinking skills in music, Mark DeTurk described good critical thinkers in music as those who can

> ...rely upon conceptual musical evidence as the basis for their evaluations...they critically evaluate a particular work by understanding the music and the merits of its parts and its totality... in this way evaluation is derived from musical evidence rather than from peer pressure, whim, or fashion.
>
> (1989, p. 22)

In DeTurk's view, critical thinkers in music must first understand the elements of music. Second, they must possess a storehouse of musical experiences so that they are enabled to make thoughtful comparisons between and among works of music. Finally, critical thinkers must possess a metacognitive strategy or disposition; they must wish to, as well as know how to, make critical musical decisions. DeTurk proposed that music instruction that teaches for critical thinking must address each of these characteristics.

Wanda May (1989) and Mildred Beane (1989) presented detailed discussions that defined and described thinking in the arts and, specifically, music. May described musical "experts" as engaging in several activities:

> ...they compose music; perform as musicians or vocalists; conduct others in the performance and interpretation of music; know how to appreciate music created by others; make informed judgments about musical works; arrange and orchestrate music for others to interpret and perform; or, through criticism, engage others in the examination of particular music forms or trends and the value of these forms or trends in social and historical contexts.
>
> (pp. 84–85)

May further recommended that music students should be:

> ...engaged in activities that promote their abilities to analyze the structural content of music by responding to elements, principles, or other sensory qualities in these forms; perceive and interpret symbolic or expressive subtleties (mood or feeling) in musical forms; and become aware of their own and others' perceptions, responses, feelings, and interpretations of musical forms.
>
> (p. 80)

According to May, the social and historical contexts of music are necessary knowledge bases for critical thinking in music. Additionally, critical thinkers in music must possess the ability to participate in effective musical criticism, defined as, "evaluating the effectiveness, worth, or success in generating specific responses to musical forms" (p. 82). In her view, critical thinking in music should not be taught in isolation, as a separate musical activity; it is best employed as a continuing exercise throughout the music curriculum. May's perspective is reminiscent of Comprehensive Musicianship through Performance (Thomas, 1970) and previews curriculum integration as an important teaching dimension.

While Beane (1989) did not present a taxonomy of musical thinking skills, she proposed a set of critical thinking skills for the arts. These were: (a) metacognition, (b) epistemic cognition (the examination of another person's thinking processes), (c) classification, (d) comparison and contrast, (e) pattern recognition, (f) causal relationships, (g) making connections, (h) identifying the main idea, (i) sequencing,

(j) developing criteria for judgment, and (k) synthesis. What makes this set of skills unique is the inclusion of epistemic cognition and pattern recognition. By epistemic cognition, we mean thinking from different musical or dialogical perspectives (Paul, 1984). Pattern recognition is another specific skill that is essential to the arts. Particularly in music, the recognition of patterns is key to understanding musical structures and forms.

As the music education profession began to define and describe critical thinking in music, some researchers were examining thinking in music as a reflective process. Paul Woodford (1997) presented a view of critical thinking derived from Dewey's concept of reflective thinking (1933). He proposed that there were four inseparable general thinking skills embedded in his thinking process of musical reflection: (1) musical observation, (2) judgment, (3) analysis and synthesis, and (4) musical imagination. In this sense, Woodford's examination of musical thinking combined social and cognitive factors that moved closer to a holistic approach. In summary, critical thinking has two broad components: abilities needed to think critically, and habits of mind that include attitudes, dispositions, values that signal intellectual independence and humility (Richardson & Whitaker, 1992).

Early 21st Century Concepts

The work described in the preceding section laid the foundation for a continued reexamination of thinking in music. In her chapter on critical thinking in *The New Handbook of Research on Music Teaching and Learning* (2002), Betty Anne Younker summarized findings from previous researchers on this topic and its relationship to music education. Important for the current discussion is the focus on critical thinking as a framework for musical thinking. Younker identified several issues that influenced how researchers and scholars thought about critical thinking in music. One was defining critical thinking in terms of specific skills which included attitudes and values. Another was the question of generalizability or how much thinking skills transfer from one discipline to another. As explored later in this chapter, both ideas relate to the fundamental approach that serves as a basis for the new Model for Holistic Musical Thinking. This approach is broader in scope and does not limit musical thinking to cognition, but rather

Table 3.1 Summary of Critical Thinking Skills in Music

Level	Thinking Skill
1.	Assuming the role of another person
2.	Classifying
3.	Comparing and contrasting
4.	Recognizing patterns
5.	Understanding causal relationships
6.	Making connections
7.	Identifying main ideas
8.	Sequencing
9.	Developing criteria for judgment
10.	Synthesizing
11.	Understanding your own thought processes

Source: Brophy (2000).

offers a more inclusive and broader understanding of the knowledge and skills needed to make and teach music.

Several researchers continued important work on critical thinking in music education in the 1980s and 1990s, as described by the conceptions and taxonomies of musical thinking they developed from 2000–2010. With the publication and widespread adoption of the National Standards for Music (Consortium of National Arts Education Associations, 1994) in the 1990s and 2000s, a growing need for valid, reliable assessment of musical knowledge and skills led some researchers and practitioners to conceive of musical thinking in new ways. Timothy Brophy (2000) adapted Beane's (1989) critical thinking processes for music, clarifying them so that teachers could better apply them in teaching practice and assessment. See Table 3.1 for those 11 skills, presented as a hierarchy of critical thinking in music.

Scott Shuler (2008) developed a model of the artistic processes in music that served as the foundation for Connecticut's Beginning Educator Support and Training program. Embedded within the artistic processes of performing, creating, and responding were the sequential activities of imagining, planning, selecting, analyzing, interpreting, rehearsing, evaluating, refining, and presenting. Musical thinking skills underlie these processes, and Shuler's conception served as a precursor to the current National Core Arts Standards (National Coalition for Core Arts Standards, 2015) and their corresponding Model Cornerstone Assessments (Burrack & Parkes, 2018).

Table 3.2 Summary of Core Competencies Model

Level	Artistic Processes	Description
1.	Capture	To know
2.	Connect	To understand
3.	Utilize	To do
4.	Analyze	To examine
5.	Create	To reflect and construct
6.	Evaluate	To critique

Source: Hartenberger (2008).

Aurelia Hartenberger (2008) presented a comprehensive alignment of musical thinking processes with existing taxonomies of cognitive, affective, and psychomotor skills. Arguing that standards and assessment are best connected through her Core Competencies Model, she developed an expanded view based on Bloom's earlier cognitive taxonomy (Anderson et al., 2001). This led to a model of sequential artistic processing which ranged from capturing at the lowest level to evaluating at the highest level. See Table 3.2 for a display of those six steps.

Hartenberger aligned levels of complexity in artistic processing and the hierarchy of conscious processes needed to apply knowledge from affective and psychomotor dimensions (Krathwohl et al., 1973; Simpson, 1972). The connections she made constitute the most complete combination of these ideas and serve as a basis for our understanding of musical thinking, feeling, and doing. As explored in the next sections of this chapter, combining the corresponding learning dimensions into one model allows us to better define and describe the multi-faceted experience of musical thinking.

Subsequent investigations into the ways different experts think have articulated perspectives on a variety of professional fields in *Exploring Signature Pedagogies: Approaches to Teaching Disciplinary Habits of Mind* (Gurung et al., 2009). For example, to prepare student-musicians to understand, value, and perform on a professional level, collegiate curricula have separate but integrated courses in music theory and history. To achieve the goal of educating a whole musician, however, "both [kinds of courses] are crucial to knowing, thinking, and doing music..." (Don et al., 2009, p. 81). This perspective offers further support for a holistic approach to music education in that it authentically connects the three learning dimensions to curricula for preparing whole musicians as professionals.

A New Pedagogical Model for Holistic Musical Thinking

In contrast to the earlier ideas of musical thinking discussed above, a new pedagogical Model for Holistic Musical Thinking represents a new direction in music education. Related to previous research, this model combines cognitive, affective, and psychomotor learning with measures of interdisciplinary pedagogy and a scale of musical engagement. This model frames the complex tasks of teaching and learning music with multiple parameters. While not all-inclusive, this model combines existing approaches into one framework that accommodates a wide range of teaching and learning experiences in music.

This pedagogical Model for Holistic Musical Thinking has five dimensions organized into two domains or focus areas. The cognitive, affective, and psychomotor dimensions address features of learning while the curriculum integration and learner engagement dimensions pertain to teaching practices. This model is holistic in several ways. As these five dimensions combine to form one model, they present a holistic view of musical thinking that includes both learner and teacher roles. By embracing the range of learning dimensions, this model also considers the whole of the learner's experience and two important teaching dimensions. See Figure 3.1 for a display of these five dimensions, arranged in the two domains.

This new direction in music education conceives of musical thinking in a holistic way to encompass the three traditional psychological learning dimensions (cognition, affect, and psychomotor) along with two teaching dimensions (curriculum integration and learner engagement). As such, this model draws its roots in actual musical practice (making music) and reflection about musical experiences. This approach to musical thinking also highlights the immediate and visceral experience of music – one which engages listeners cognitively, emotionally, and physically. Whether it be a Sousa march or a Gaelic lullaby, music has the power to engage both listeners and performers with mental imagery, voluntary and involuntary sympathetic movement, and their related feelings. As such, the embodiment of music is one of its distinguishing and defining features (Smith, 2022).

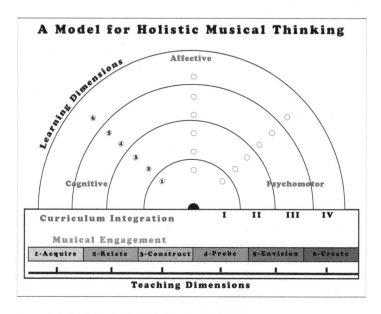

Figure 3.1 A Model for Holistic Musical Thinking.

Three Learning Dimensions

Music learning sits at the nexus of cognitive, affective, and psycho-motor learning. While not superior to any other form of learning, music learning is in the position of drawing on the three well-established dimensions of learning as supportive pillars. In the model, each of the three dimensions is distinct yet musical experiences regularly rely on all three modes of learning. By virtue of its multi-faceted impact on performers and audiences alike, we may best define and describe musical learning as the intersection of cognitive, psychomotor, and affective learning.

The idea of combining taxonomies to embrace the multi-faceted experiences of student-musicians appeared in the early 21st century. For example, Frank Abrahams suggested this confluence of ideas in his Critical Pedagogy for Music Education or CPME (2005, 2007). He described music lessons that, "...pose and solve problems that engage children in critical thinking, critical action, and critical feeling" (2007, p. 1). Learning theories that Abrahams cited highlight the diversity of learning styles while promoting a constructivist approach that celebrates student discovery (2007). Perhaps the most important of CPME for our discussion of holistic musical thinking is the notion that musicians routinely engage in a combination of thinking, feeling, and doing as genuine music-making or musicking. More recently, his example lesson plans describe learning goals that include understanding (cognitive), encountering (experiential), meaningful (constructivist), and doing (behavioral) objectives (Abrahams, 2023). In this way, a holistic approach to musical thinking is not only a more inclusive but also a more authentic representation of musical experiences.

Combining the three learning dimensions is convincing not only from a theoretical perspective but also a scientific one. As Donald Hodges and Wilfried Grun wrote, "two extremely important aspects for education come from brain research: the involvement of the body and movement in the learning process and the role of emotion and motivation" (2018, p. 214). In their insightful review of the related neuroscience literature, they also explain that there is no "music center" in the brain; rather, musical experiences can enhance the size and function of several brain structures including the auditory cortex, corpus callosum, cerebellum, sensorimotor cortex, and gray and white matter. While a detailed discussion of these connections is beyond the scope of this book, recognizing them provides empirical evidence to support a more holistic approach to music teaching and learning.

Two Teaching Dimensions

The teaching domain is comprised of two dimensions: curricular integration and musical engagement. All curriculum integration is not equal. The relative quality of curriculum integration depends on the balance of teaching and learning in music and in any other disciplines. Far too often, teachers teach their students to sing about frogs or colors in the rainbow and call it "integration." For example, while "The Fifty Nifty United States" (Charles, 1961) is a catchy and informative choral anthem, simply using this music does not integrate the music and Social Studies or History curricula. What completes the integration between the two subjects is an intentional and thoughtful learning connection, based on the learning standards or student learning outcomes for *both* disciplines.

This five-dimensional Model for Holistic Musical Thinking contains both teaching and learning dimensions. The model displays the two fundamental components in education (teaching and learning) on two intersecting planes: cognitive, affective, and psychomotor learning together with curricular integration and musical engagement. As shown, the learning and teaching dimensions are not mutually exclusive; their intersection shows the holistic nature of musical experiences.

By considering the impact of musical experiences in terms of each of these dimensions side-by-side, the model provides a holistic view from a well-rounded and inclusive perspective. Simply put, memorable musical events have an emotional impact on the participants. At the same time, understanding the related history and structure of any musical experience adds to its appreciation and enjoyment. Finally, the act of responding physically to music as a listener, or actually making the music as a performer, provides another layer of experience that literally moves people to the music (Benson, 2011).

The teaching dimensions are measures of curriculum integration. From discipline-specific to transdisciplinary, these dimensions indicate how connected or independent the learning outcomes are with respect to other disciplines. See Table 3.3 for a listing of the four levels of curriculum integration in this model.

Comparatively, a discipline-specific lesson treats music independently from other subjects. It has no intentional connection to learning goals in other areas. Supportive curricula provide connections in which music enhances student learning of terms and concepts from other areas. An interdisciplinary curriculum demonstrates ways in which learning common to music and other disciplines is important to and expressed in both contexts. Transdisciplinary curricula treat music and another discipline with co-equal importance and provide for more

Table 3.3 Levels of Curriculum Integration

Level	Name	Description
I	Discipline Specific	Music learning is distinctly separate from other disciplines
II	Supportive	Music enhances learning in another discipline
III	Interdisciplinary	Learning in music and another discipline are equally important
IV	Transdisciplinary	Boundaries between music and another discipline blur

holistic experiences (Drake & Reid, 2021). In the fullest sense, this type of curriculum blurs boundaries between disciplines to fuse the learning experience. Resources for lesson planning and longer-term instruction can aid teachers in adding or enhancing their curricular integration practices. For examples see: "Meaningful Connections in a Comprehensive Approach to the Music Curriculum," in *Music and Music Education in People's Lives* (Barrett & Veblen, 2018); *Music in Childhood* (Campbell & Scott-Kassner, 2019); and *Integrating Music across the Elementary Curriculum* (Harney, 2020).

A Taxonomy of Musical Engagement. In review, taxonomies consist of hierarchical levels, displaying the relationship between their components. As defined in the previous chapter, taxonomies are useful tools to guide teachers in structuring learning outcomes and targets for their students. In addition, each level builds upon the previous one and assumes achievement at the previous levels. This section presents a taxonomy for musical engagement as part of the Model for Holistic Musical Thinking, shown in Figure 3.1. Just as the other taxonomies pertain to cognitive, affective, and psychomotor dimensions of learning, this taxonomy applies to music teaching and indicates levels of intended learner engagement with musical behaviors. See Figure 3.2 for a display of the taxonomy of musical engagement levels. Table 3.4 presents the same taxonomy in an expanded form with descriptors for the three learning dimensions.

The Taxonomy of Musical Engagement expands on an unpublished taxonomy focused on music cognition (Johnson & Brophy, 2014), and here connects with affective and psychomotor processes. As compared to separate taxonomies, these holistic connections more completely reflect the multi-modal and multi-dimensional phenomena of making and experiencing music. Additional scholarship on educating whole musicians through meaningful and transformative learning offers a

1 Acquire	2 Relate	3 Construct	4 Probe	5 Envision	6 Create
• Notice • Receive • Observe	• Compare • Respond • Connect	• Assign meaning • Make sense • Practice actions	• Explore ideas • Examine • Explore actions	• Formulate ideas • Imagine • Solve	• Compose • Verify • Perform

Figure 3.2 Taxonomy of Musical Engagement.

Table 3.4 Levels of Musical Engagement with Example Learning Processes

Level	Description	Example Learning Processes		
		Cognitive	*Affective*	*Psychomotor*
1	Acquire	Notice	Receive	Observe
2	Relate	Compare with prior knowledge	Respond to previous experiences	Connect with learned actions
3	Construct	Assign meaning	Make sense	Practice actions
4	Probe	Explore ideas	Examine perspectives	Solve problems
5	Envision	Formulate new ideas	Imagine possibilities	Explore actions
6	Create	Edit and compose	Verify perceptions	Perform new techniques

major paradigm shift and further validates this holistic approach to musical thinking (O'Neill, 2018).

The experience of music is time-bound and therefore rooted in the physical world. Because making music is an intensely physical task, how the mind and body interact is an important and emergent trend in learning research, with important implications for music teaching (Hodges & Grun, 2018; Kronland-Martinet et al., 2016). This combination of cognitive, emotional, and behavioral experiences, or embodiment (Lux et al., 2021), is important to a holistic view of musical thinking because it provides a multi-faceted understanding that literally moves and touches casual listeners and professional musicians alike. Regarding the body as an instrument elevates the psychomotor dimension to the same level as cognitive and affective learning (Benson, 2011). It also honors knowledge held in and by the body (Winter, 2013) while inviting thoughtful and philosophical explorations of music education (Smith, 2022).

The purpose of music education is sustained, lifelong musical engagement (Pitts, 2017) and begins with engaging, multi-faceted instructional experiences in music. Engagement is about learner agency and opportunity to grow. Its purpose is also to empower or amplify musicianship, on both the part of the student and the teacher (Abrahams, 2023). Making music, or musicking, is also about developing musical identities, as people find and make meaning through musical engagement. When understood beyond merely gaining information, engaged learning experiences are transformative and involve the whole person (Wells, 2000) and lead toward musical independence (Boardman, 1989).

The foundation for musical engagement uses an asset instead of a deficit approach. Identifying and growing competencies, for example, is a key first step to empower learners and foster their own self-expression (O'Neill, 2018). From an instructional perspective, the focus is on building confidence and resiliency to result in sustained musical engagement (O'Neill, 2011). Therefore, a transformative musical engagement includes these key elements:

- Teaching begins with student knowledge.
- Skills, knowledge, and voices developed from engagement in the activity.
- Teaching and learning are both individual and collaborative processes.
- Teaching and learning are transformative processes.

(O'Neill, 2018, pp. 177–178)

Similar to the way Hartenberger (2008) aligned the affective and psychomotor dimensions with six artistic processes, this five-dimensional model for holistic musical thinking categorizes cognitive, affective, and psychomotor skills into six levels. Each of these is interdependent, yet musicians may not necessarily achieve parallel levels in each dimension.

An Example Vignette

By considering the following vignette or account of an example classroom episode, we can better understand how to apply the Model for Holistic Musical Thinking in a practical setting.

Mrs. Drexel's fifth-grade students file in for their weekly general music class and immediately begin to chat among themselves when they see the arrangement of measuring tapes, clipboards, and sets of boom whackers laid out. This is by design because Mrs. Drexel has planned an integrated lesson combining mathematics and music. She begins by quieting the class and taking attendance. Once complete, she asks the students if they remember their previous work with boom whackers (colored, hollow plastic tubes of different lengths that resonate with different pitches when struck on a hard surface). Nearly all the students respond with an enthusiastic "Yes, of course. Those were so fun last year!" Today, Mrs. Drexel explains, they will use the boom whackers to connect music with math. Despite hearing a few groans, she proceeds to begin with a counting activity.

Mrs. Drexel asks students to count with her, "1 2 3 4, 1 2 3 4…" Her students respond without hesitation while she then adds body percussion, tapping her feet on each count. The students imitate her on cue. Once secure, Mrs. Drexel stops the students to introduce a new motion. She slides her hand down her arm to make a smooth motion for counts 1, 2, 3, and 4. She invites the students to join in rhythm. Once secure, she stops the class and reviews the two body percussion patterns. Then, she divides the class into two groups, with one group tapping their feet for every count, while the other group makes the four-count continuous motion. After some repetition, she has the groups switch parts.

Then, Mrs. Drexel stops the class and asks, "Instead of my arm motion, if I play a long, sustained sound on this long red boom whacker with a long scrape, which smaller boom whacker should we use to play for the clapping part?" After some discussion, the students come to the realization that the smaller boom whacker should be one quarter of the larger length. "Ah, I see," Mrs. Drexel says, "The ratio of the first beat to the smaller or subdivided beats is 1 to 4. Let's see which smaller boom whacker is the best fit." Working in small groups, the students measure the larger boom whacker and divide that length by four. They then find the closest fit from the other available boom whackers to show that 1:4 ratio.

Using the measuring tapes, the students discover that the long red boom whacker (50 inches in length) is four times the length of the short blue boom whacker (12.5 inches in length).

Projecting instructions from her computer on an overhead screen, Mrs. Drexel gives the students their first task: substitute the long red and short blue boom whackers for the body percussion patterns and perform the same rhythm patterns, being sure to listen for the ratio of 1:4. Despite the major-ninth dissonance between the long red (low C) and short blue (high B) boom whackers, the students work through the assignment as their teacher circulates and gives either praise or feedback. After regaining their attention, Mrs. Drexel distributes the clipboards and gives them a different assignment: with a partner,

Boom Whacker	Color	Length
C		
D		
E		
F		
G		
A		
B		
C'		

Figure 3.3 Boom Whacker Length Chart.

identify each boom whacker by color and letter, then measure its length to complete the chart shown in Figure 3.3.

Once complete, each pair of students chooses two differently sized boom whackers and calculates the ratio or size differential between them. As Mrs. Drexel suggests, they may do this on paper (with numbers) or hands-on, with the instruments. The students then play the ratio they have found (for example, 1:2 or 1:5). Mrs. Drexel circulates around her classroom and either corrects or complements the students' work. To complete this teaching episode, Mrs. Drexel collects the clipboards and chart papers before having the students find new partners for the last activity. She has them respond to two reflective questions, displayed on her overhead screen:

- How difficult or easy were the activities today?
- What did you learn about how math and music are similar?
- How difficult or easy was it for you to work with other students?

The students discuss with their partners for several minutes while Mrs. Drexel circulates and answers any questions the students have. To end, she asks for volunteers to share any ideas from their pair-sharing. She offers feedback or confirmation for each volunteer as the class concludes.

In summary, Mrs. Drexel engaged her students at the fourth or Probe level by using an integrated lesson plan, combining math and music learning. She combined psychomotor skills (body percussion) with an understanding of ratio and measurement, appropriate for their grade level. In addition to the cognitive aspect of mathematical measurement (by comparing and dividing), she also ended the class with a

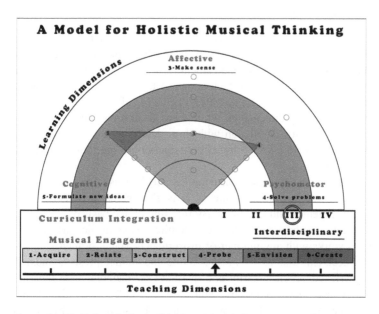

Figure 3.4 Holistic Musical Thinking Model for an Example Vignette, General Music.

set of self-reflective questions. Students considered their interpersonal learning as well as how the disciplines of math and music connected. See Figure 3.4 for a display of the teaching and learning dimensions used in this example vignette.

As shown in this example, the level of curriculum integration matches the level of cognitive, affective, and psychomotor learning. In turn, those inform the overall level of musical engagement. The shaded quadrilateral outlines each level of learning by dimension and indicates the corresponding level of musical engagement. Mrs. Drexel could use this information to increase her focus on affective and psychomotor learning outcomes. While not deficient, learning in those two dimensions was less of a priority than cognitive outcomes. She could also recognize that a more subject-specific approach may be more appropriate when teaching performance skills or addressing attitudes and feelings about music. More holistically, Mrs. Drexel could consider the level of musical engagement she intended for this lesson and consider ways to modify the activities to advance toward the Envision or Create levels, amplifying her students' musicality.

Summary

The Model for Holistic Musical Thinking leads to musical independence, a long-term goal of many music teachers and teacher-educators. The model also reflects engagement as a demonstration of sustained participation and focus, which is one of the main purposes of music education. The model integrates cognitive, affective, and psychomotor learning dimensions while also illustrating ways to connect interdisciplinary instruction with those learning outcomes, resulting in a corresponding measure of participation on the musical engagement taxonomy.

The model captures musical authenticity because it reflects musical engagement in musical contexts. It is also inclusive of contrasting musical genres and traditions. By focusing on the basis of perceiving and interpreting sounds, the model applies to any musical tradition. It also works with any number of instrumental, vocal, or technological musical expressions of music. While the model presents musical experiences as necessarily and qualitatively different than those of other disciplines, innovative educators can make cross-disciplinary connections in ways that support learning. Those may take the form of supportive curricular connections, interdisciplinary parallels, or new transdisciplinary inventions. In any case, both learners and teachers can see themselves within this model, constructed with both the teacher and learner in mind.

As the following chapter details, the Model for Holistic Musical Thinking in action shows applications of these ideas in K-12 settings. It also explores different levels of musical engagement while illustrating those within three variations on the same vignettes. As such, we notice the variety of musical thinking that teachers can facilitate through these vignettes. While no one variation or level along the teaching and learning dimensions is better than another, more involved levels of curriculum integration necessarily involve higher order thinking processes (Harney, 2020).

References

Abrahams, F. (2005). Transforming classroom music instruction with ideas from critical pedagogy. *Music Educators Journal, 92*(1), 62–67.

Abrahams, F. (2007). Critical pedagogy for music education: A best practice to prepare future music educators. *Visions of Research in Music Education, 7*(10) https://digitalcommons.lib.uconn.edu/vrme/vol7/iss1/10

Abrahams, F. (2023). Critical pedagogy. In F. Abrahams (Ed.), *A music pedagogy for our time* (pp. 13–40). GIA Publications, Inc.

Anderson, L. W., Krathwohl, D. R., Airasian, P. W., Cruikshank, K. A., Mayer, R. E., Pintrich, P. R., Raths, J., & Wittrock, M. C. (Eds.) (2001). *A taxonomy for learning, teaching, and assessing - A revision of Bloom's taxonomy of educational objectives.* Addison Wesley Longman, Inc.

Barrett, J. R., & Veblen, K. K. (2018). Meaningful connections in a comprehensive approach to the music curriculum. In G. E. McPherson, & G. F. Welch (Eds.), *Music and music education in people's lives: An Oxford handbook of music education, Volume 2* (pp. 141–159). Oxford University Press.

Beane, M. (1989). Focus on fine arts, ED 317 477. Educational Resources Information Center.

Benson, B. E. (2011). Phenomenology of music. In T. Gracyk & A. Kania (Eds.), *The Routledge companion to philosophy and music* (pp. 581–591). Routledge.

Bernard, C. F. (2023). Critical thinking, feeling, and action. In F. Abrahams (Ed.), *A music pedagogy for our time* (pp. 173–200). GIA Publications, Inc.

Boardman, E. (Ed.). (1989). *Dimensions of musical thinking.* MENC - The National Association for Music Education.

Brophy, T. S. (2000). *Assessing the developing child musician.* GIA Publications, Inc.

Burrack, F., & Parkes, K. A. (Eds.). (2018). *Applying Model Cornerstone Assessments in K–12 music: A research-supported approach.* Rowman & Littlefield.

Campbell, P. S., & Scott-Kassner, C. (2019). *Music in childhood enhanced: From preschool through the elementary grades.* Cengage Learning.

Charles, R. (1961). *Fifty-nifty United States.* Roncom Music Company.

Consortium of National Arts Education Associations. (1994). *National standards for arts education: What every young American should know and be able to do in the arts.* MENC - the National Association for Music Education.

DeTurk, M. (1989). Critical and creative thinking in music. In E. Boardman (Ed.), *Dimensions of musical thinking* (pp. 21–32). MENC.

Dewey, J. (1933). *How we think.* D.C.L. Heath.

Don, G., Garvey, C., & Sadeghpour, M. (2009). Theory and practice: Signature pedagogies in music theory and performance. In R. A. Gurung, N. L. Chick, & A. Haynie, A. (Eds.), *Exploring signature pedagogies: Approaches to teaching disciplinary habits of mind* (pp. 81–98). Stylus Publishing.

Drake, S., & Reid, J. (2021). Thinking now: Transdisciplinary thinking as a disposition. *Academia Letters*, 1–6.

Freire, P. (1970/2000). *Pedagogy of the oppressed.* Bloomsbury.

Gurung, R. A., Chick, N. L., & Haynie, A. (2009). *Exploring signature pedagogies: Approaches to teaching disciplinary habits of mind.* Stylus Publishing.

Harney, K. (2020). *Integrating music across the elementary curriculum.* Oxford University Press.

Hartenberger, A. (2008). Connecting assessments to standards through core conceptual competencies. In T. S. Brophy (Ed.), *Assessment in music education: Integrating curriculum, theory, and practice* (pp. 71–89). GIA Publications.

Hodges, D. A., & Grun, W. (2018). Implications of neurosciences and brain research for music teaching and learning. In G. E. McPherson, & G. F. Welch (Eds.), *Music and music education in people's lives: An Oxford handbook of music education, Volume 1* (pp. 206–224). Oxford University Press.

Hoque, M. E. (2016). Three domains of learning: Cognitive, affective and psychomotor. *The Journal of EFL Education and Research, 2*(2), 45–52.

Johnson, D. C., & Brophy, T. S. (2013). *Critical thinking in music education.* [Unpublished manuscript].

Johnson, D. C., & Brophy, T. S. (2014). *A taxonomy of musical thinking.* [Unpublished manuscript].

Krathwohl, D. R., Bloom, B. S., & Masia, B. B. (1973). *Taxonomy of educational objectives, the classification of educational goals. Handbook II: Affective domain.* David McKay Co., Inc.

Kronland-Martinet, R., Aramaki, M., & Ystad, S. (Eds.). (2016). *Music, mind, and embodiment.* Springer.

Lux, V., Non, A. L., Pexman, P. M., Stadler, W., Weber, L. A., & Krüger, M. (2021). A developmental framework for embodiment research: the next step toward integrating concepts and methods. *Frontiers in Systems Neuroscience, 15,* https://doi.org/10.3389/fnsys.2021.672740

Marzano, R. J., Brandt, R. S., Hughes, C. S., Jones, B. F., Presseisen, B. Z., Rankin, S. C., & Suhor, C. (1988). *Dimensions of thinking: A framework for curriculum and instruction.* Association for Curriculum Supervision and Instruction.

May, W. T. (1989). Understanding and critical thinking in elementary art and music: General Subjects Center series no. 8, ED308 982. Educational Resources Information Center.

National Coalition for Core Arts Standards. (2015). *National Core Arts Standards.* State Education Agency Directors of Arts Education.

O'Neill, S. A. (2011). Learning in and through music performance: Understanding cultural diversity via inquiry and dialogue. In M. Barrett (Ed.), *A cultural psychology for music education* (pp. 179–200). Oxford University Press.

O'Neill, S. A. (2018). Becoming a music learner: Toward a theory of transformative music engagement. In G. E. McPherson, & G. F. Welch (Eds.),

Music and music education in people's lives: An Oxford handbook of music education, Volume 1 (pp. 163–186). Oxford University Press.

Paul, R. (1984). Critical thinking: Fundamental to education for a free society. *Educational Researcher, 48,* 4–14.

Pitts, S. E. (2017). What is music education for? Understanding and fostering routes into lifelong musical engagement. *Music Education Research, 19*(2), 160–168. https://www.tandfonline.com/doi/abs/10.1080/14613 808.2016.1166196

Richardson, C. P., & Whitaker, N. P. (1992). Critical thinking and music education. In R. Colwell (Ed.), *Handbook of research on music teaching and learning* (pp. 546–560). Schirmer Books.

Shuler, S. (2008). Large-Scale assessment of music performance: Some whys and hows for today's data-driven educational environment. In T. S. Brophy (Ed.), *Assessment in music education: Integrating curriculum, theory, and practice* (pp. 123–137). GIA Publications, Inc.

Simpson, E. J. (1972). *The classification of educational objectives in the psychomotor domain.* Gryphon House.

Smith, G. D. (2022). *A philosophy of playing drum kit: magical nexus.* Cambridge University Press.

Thomas, R. B. (1970). Rethinking the curriculum. *Music Educators Journal, 56*(6), 68–70.

Trilling, B., & Fadel, C. (2009). *21st century skills: Learning for life in our times.* John Wiley & Sons.

Wells, G. (2000). Dialogic inquiry in education: Building on the legacy of Vygotsky. In C. D. Lee & P. Smagorinsky (Eds.), *Vygotskian perspectives on literacy research: Constructing meaning through collaborative inquiry* (pp. 51–85). Cambridge University Press.

Winter, R. (2013). Language, empathy, archetype: Action-metaphors of the transcendental in musical experience. *Philosophy of Music Education Review, 21*(2), 103–119.

Woodford, P. (1997). Transfer in music as social and reconstructive inquiry. In Rideout, R. (Ed.), *On the sociology of music education, 43–54.* University of Oklahoma.

Younker, B. A (2002). Critical thinking. In R. Colwell, & C. Richardson (Eds.), *The new handbook of research on music teaching and learning* (pp. 162–170). Oxford University Press.

4 Practical Applications

The Model in Action

As a result of a long-standing dichotomy in education, there is often a stark contrast between theory and practice. This difference is one that challenges both academic scholars and K-12 practitioners alike. One advantage in the translation from idea to action, or from theory to practice, is that the classroom applications keep concepts well-grounded in school realities. To address the need to align the two in clear and practical ways (Colwell & Webster, 2011), this chapter presents the Model for Holistic Musical Thinking in action. We consider three example lessons presented as classroom vignettes to illustrate the model with specific content and typical music education settings. While this book is not a teacher's guide, some examples of practical applications serve to illustrate the utility of this model followed by a framework for developing a musical thinking curriculum, and implications of the model for the future.

In this chapter, we move "on stage" with three variations of three exemplar lessons that demonstrate all teaching and learning dimensions of the model in action. The following three vignettes demonstrate how educators could use the model to evaluate the scope of a lesson, in three different variations for three typical music classrooms: general music, choral music, and instrumental music. Each lesson offers a variety of cognitive, affective, and psychomotor learning outcomes. The lessons also present a range of teaching approaches: interdisciplinary vs. subject-specific, and points on the musical engagement scale. Taken together, they present a range of teaching and learning profiles aligned with the Model for Holistic Musical Thinking.

DOI: 10.4324/9780429270383-4

Before looking into these example classes, we may ask ourselves: why should we measure teaching and learning dimensions? What are the benefits of quantifying and assessing such flexible and personal experiences as teaching and learning music? In other words, why bother assessing music teaching and learning? One advantage is to organize our thoughts and strategies around pertinent domains so that we can know and do more than we otherwise could (Bruner, 1997). As we see in these vignettes, the model in action also offers us the chance to critically reflect on contrasting teaching and learning strategies. While none of the models are better or worse than another, they do present varying levels of musical engagement as characterized by the teaching and learning dimensions. Another reason is that hierarchies apply to musical understanding as well as any other discipline. In fact, "Our minds seem particularly adept at (and even inclined toward) forming hierarchies out of musical materials" (Larson, 2012, p. 51). Another key point is that the affective taxonomy (Krathwohl et al., 1973) has directly shaped the role of emotion in education. More specifically, this taxonomy "…looks at the process of forming and internalizing values….The student that attaches value to music or music learning will be more likely to persist" (Letts, 2018, p. 290). Therefore, as shown by recent advances in the field of music education assessment (Brophy, 2019), we can learn insightful lessons about our own musical learning and values by taking an analytical view of the music teaching and learning processes. As an additional practical application, see the Appendix of this book for a Model of Holistic Musical Thinking as a worksheet. After mapping lessons plans onto this infographic, consider ways to enhance the level of musical engagement by adjusting the other teaching and learning dimensions.

Classroom Vignettes: On Stage

This chapter begins with three variations of three vignettes presented as ways to consider different levels of musical engagement along the K-12 grade spectrum and in contrasting musical settings. In addition to sequences of events in example classrooms, these vignettes describe example lessons and student-teacher interactions. To support their validity in terms of standards and application throughout the United States, each lesson also aligns with the National Core Arts Standards (2015) and the Model Cornerstone Assessments (Burrack & Parkes, 2018). The intention of this analysis is to show how music teachers

Table 4.1 Levels of Musical Engagement with Example Learning Processes

Level	Description	Example Learning Processes		
		Cognitive	*Affective*	*Psychomotor*
1	Acquire	Notice	Receive	Observe
2	Relate	Compare with prior knowledge	Respond to previous experiences	Connect with learned actions
3	Construct	Assign meaning	Make sense	Practice actions
4	Probe	Explore ideas	Examine perspectives	Solve problems
5	Envision	Formulate new ideas	Imagine possibilities	Explore actions
6	Create	Edit and compose	Verify perceptions	Perform new techniques

and teacher-educators can apply the Model for Holistic Musical Thinking in their classrooms. While not valuing one type of learning or one level of teaching over another (Hallmark, 2012), we explore how this model translates into practical teaching vignettes.

In keeping with the scope and purpose of this chapter, the three vignettes presented in this chapter provide important practical examples of ways to apply the model, emphasizing critical and reflective thinking (Conway, 1999). In addition, three variations of each vignette illustrate a range of possible teaching and learning approaches. At each grade range (elementary, middle, and high school), the different teaching and learning levels in variations 2 and 3 are extensions of variation 1. Corresponding infographics of the model illustrate the variety of teaching and learning dimensions for each variation. As a reminder, Table 4.1 displays the six levels of musical engagement with corresponding cognitive, affective, and psychomotor processes.

For reference, Table 4.2 displays the four levels of curriculum integration with descriptors as used in the following vignettes.

Vignette One: Elementary General Music

Variation 1. Mrs. Álvarez begins her third-grade general music class with a new song. The students are excited and quietly whisper to each

Table 4.2 Levels of Curriculum Integration

Level	Name	Description
I	Discipline Specific	Music learning is distinctly separate from other disciplines
II	Supportive	Music enhances learning in another discipline
III	Interdisciplinary	Learning in music and another discipline are equally important
IV	Transdisciplinary	Boundaries between music and another discipline blur

other before their teacher calls their attention to a display of a pancake cooking on a stove. She asks what the students see and either affirms or gently guides their responses as they share attitudes and their impressions of the display. The students discuss eating pancakes, and other favorite breakfast options. She focuses the students' attention on the pancake as the topic of the new song. She then reads Christina Rossetti's poem "Mix a Pancake."

> Mix a pancake,
> Stir a pancake,
> Pop it in the pan;
> Fry the pancake,
> Toss the pancake—
> Catch it if you can.
>   (Prelutsky, 1986, p. 50)

Mrs. Álvarez asks the students what kind of voice she used – with reminders as needed about the four voice categories they learned last year: speaking, singing, whispering, and calling. Once they remember and confirm that she used a speaking voice, she has the students echo her line by line. She then shifts to her singing voice and sings the same text as a pentatonic melody, shown in Figure 4.1.

The students listen to Mrs. Álvarez sing the song several times and then demonstrate their listening skills by echo-singing after her, phrase-by-phrase. As they sing more and more of the song in response, Mrs. Álvarez listens for correct pitches and rhythms. She quizzes them with questions about the form (identifying parts or phrases) and melody

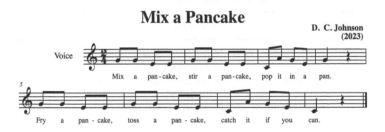

Figure 4.1 "Mix a Pancake" Melody.

(melodic contour) of the song. To assist her students with purposeful motions, she identifies specific action words in the poem (verbs) and demonstrates purposeful motions to illustrate those actions (e.g., mix, stir, and pop). The students mimic her motions as they sing the song.

Once the students have shown they know the lyrics and can sing them accurately and independently with purposeful motions, Mrs. Álvarez adds one motion to the song – she claps on the quarter rest to fill in that silence. She asks the students to observe this and copy her motions. To conclude this teaching episode, Mrs. Álvarez checks for student proficiency by having them sing and perform the motions without her assistance. See Figure 4.2 for a display of the teaching and learning dimensions used in this variation.

Variation 2. As in the first variation, Mrs. Álvarez presents the same poem aurally and then teaches the melody by rote. To alter the level of teaching and learning dimensions, she makes several changes as pedagogical extensions. Although she uses the same text, she adds questions about the meaning of this poem (e.g., Have you ever caught a pancake? Why would you need to catch it? and Do pancakes run fast?). She encourages students to consider how silly or serious this poem is, and to reflect on what the author meant.

To extend ideas in the text, Mrs. Álvarez introduces a new set of lyrics that she created for the same melody:

> Blueberry, strawberry, chocolate chip, put them on a plate;
> Pour some juice, add some syrup, they will all taste great!

She leads a discussion about the new text, asking the students to make comparisons. As they respond, she draws their attention to what the

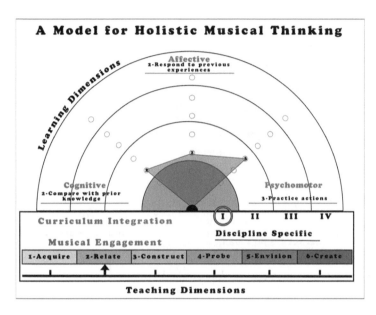

Figure 4.2 Holistic Musical Thinking Model for Vignette 1, Variation 1.

new lyrics contribute to the pancakes (e.g., flavors and being a part of a whole breakfast). To fill in the quarter rest at the end of the fourth measure, she asks the students to find a vocal sound or body percussion that would fit with the theme of the song. After allowing time for the students to experiment with some ideas, Mrs. Álvarez invites students to share and gives feedback as needed so that they fill that silent beat appropriately.

To assist her students with purposeful motions, she asks them about the action words (verbs) that they are singing. She guides the students in improvising motions to demonstrate those verbs, first individually and then with a partner. To organize their ideas, she helps the students decide on a unified version of the motions and leads them in practicing those together while they sing the song. Figure 4.3 displays the teaching and learning dimensions used in this variation of the lesson.

Variation 3. For this variation, Mrs. Álvarez begins the teaching episode by asking students to describe their favorite breakfast foods. She then extends that discussion to include any breakfast option they want (i.e., students imagine possibilities beyond their usual breakfast).

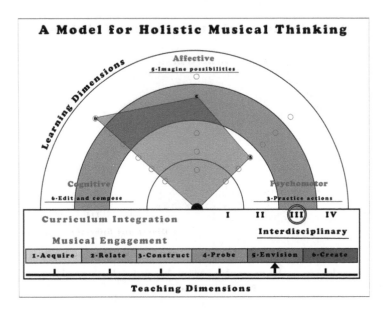

Figure 4.3 Holistic Musical Thinking Model for Vignette 1, Variation 2.

As the students share, she acknowledges their ideas and she writes key words on a white board for later reference. Then, she tells the students about one of her favorite breakfast options: pancakes! That leads into her teaching the song "Mix a Pancake" aurally as in variations 1 and 2.

Returning to the white board, she has the students read those ideas aloud with her while they keep a steady beat with body percussion (e.g., patsching or patting on their laps). She draws their attention to the number of parts in each word, which she labels as "syllables," as they speak them in rhythm (e.g., "pan-cake" having two syllables). Either in small groups or as a whole class, Mrs. Álvarez has the students use new ideas to compose their own version of the lyrics. As needed, she assists the students in fitting the new lyrics with the given melody and rhythm. To assemble their class version of this song, she asks students about what musical form they would like to use. She suggests these options: to begin and end with the original text, speak or sing original verses in between, and accompany the lyrics with the given or improvised purposeful motions. She helps the class decide on a form and then leads them in performing their version of this song

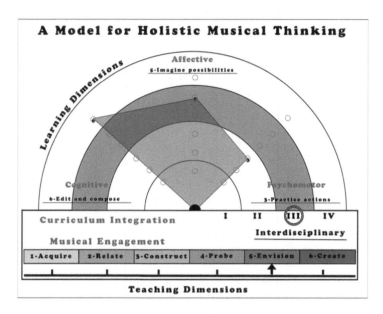

Figure 4.4 Holistic Musical Thinking Model for Vignette 1, Variation 3.

to conclude the class. See Figure 4.4 for a display of the teaching and learning dimensions used in Variation 3.

Vignette One Summary. In the first vignette, we learn how Mrs. Álvarez uses the same basic material to address similar learning objectives at different levels. These three variations have increasing higher levels of musical engagement based on the cognitive, affective, and psychomotor learning dimensions. While the student learning is more limited in the first variation, focusing on echo-singing and mimicking the teacher's motion, their roles expand in the other variations to include more student ownership and independent learning. For example, the students improvise and collectively decide on their own lyrics. They also compare alternative texts for the same melody, analyze syllables when creating original phrases, and set those in a steady beat pattern. In every variation, Mrs. Álvarez focuses on music learning outcomes but expands the level of musical engagement by increasing the range of thinking skills and curricular integration. See Table 4.3 for a summary of the learning and teaching levels for each variation.

Table 4.3 Summary of Teaching and Learning Levels in Vignette 1 for Elementary General Music

Variation	Cognitive Processing	Affective Processing	Psychomotor Processing	Curricular Integration	Musical Engagement
1	Level 2 compare with prior knowledge	Level 2 respond to previous experiences	Level 3 practice actions	Level I Discipline Specific	Level 2 Relate
2	Level 3 assign meaning	Level 3 make sense	Level 4 solve problems	Level II Supportive	Level 3 Construct
3	Level 6 edit and compose	Level 5 imagine possibilities	Level 3 practice actions	Level III Interdisciplinary	Level 5 Envision

Vignette Two: Middle School Choral Music

Variation 1. Mr. Baker welcomes his seventh-grade choir to their afternoon rehearsal. As his students arrive, they chat and jostle as they settle into their seats. To warm up, Mr. Baker uses his normal routine of scales and vocal exercises, today including exercises that outline a minor triad in preparation for the new music he will introduce, *Wayfaring Stranger* (Emerson, 2023). Before distributing the sheet music to his SA choir, he explains that they are about to begin learning a new spiritual that includes some body percussion. A few students are surprised and wonder if they will be playing drum sets. With a wink and a smile, he demonstrates the rhythmic pattern that begins this arrangement using patsching (patting) and clapping. After a few repetitions and at a slower tempo, the students respond with the body percussion in unison. See Figure 4.5 for this body percussion pattern from the sheet music.

To challenge the students kinesthetically, Mr. Baker asks them to find two different body percussion sounds that they could use to create the same rhythmic pattern. After some time for experimentation, he asks them to work with a partner on the same assignment. The singers explore different ways to show the same rhythmic pattern using snaps, claps, stomps, and fist-bumps. Then, Mr. Baker distributes the sheet music and has the students find the opening pattern in the first four measures. He asks them to study the notation and practice the pattern in the sheet music. Then, he asks them what they notice about that section. As needed, Mr. Baker either explains or confirms what details he expects students to notice: the percussion clef, the two types of percussion sounds (timbres), and the stem direction indicating those sounds. He then asks the students why the arranger used that particular pattern; what did he mean to represent by it? The answer is: a heartbeat (Emerson, 2023).

Wayfaring Stranger

Traditional Spiritual
Arr. Roger Emerson

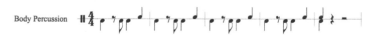

Figure 4.5 Body Percussion Pattern from "Wayfaring Stranger" (Traditional, arr. Emerson, 2023).

From behind the piano, Mr. Baker plays the initial statement of the melody. He directs the singers to read the lyrics to themselves while he sings the melody and accompanies himself. With repetition, the singers join in as they are comfortable and sing the opening statement of the melody in unison. Mr. Baker then prepares the students to listen to the professional demonstration recording provided by the publisher. He instructs them to listen for the development of the song (i.e., how the sections are organized, how it changes from section to section, and what repeats in each section). After listening, he has students respond verbally to those prompts. He offers corrections or confirmations of the students' answers, making reference to measure numbers to orient the students to the form of the overall arrangement.

Mr. Baker then asks the students to listen to the demonstration recording again, now focusing on the lyrics and following along with the sheet music. He then asks the students to consider the message of the text (i.e., what the song is about, what emotion or feeling is in the words, and how they could summarize the story of the lyrics). To encourage more interpersonal communication, Mr. Baker has students turn and talk with a partner to answer his questions. After a few minutes, he invites students to share their ideas with the class. Building on the emotional message of the lyrics and to revisit the opening body percussion, Mr. Baker concludes the class by having the choir stand and perform the opening section (singing only the melody in unison). As a preview, he directs students' attention to the harmony parts that they will start learning at the next rehearsal. See Figure 4.6 for a display of the teaching and learning dimensions used in this variation.

Variation 2. In variation 2, Mr. Baker does not spend time exploring different body percussion patterns or listening to a recording of *Wayfaring Stranger* (Emerson, 2023). Instead, he uses more traditional techniques to teach notes and rhythms to the singers by voice part. For example, he teaches the countermelody section by rote. Beginning in measure 13, the sopranos learn this part and then add it to the repeated melodic line in the alto voice.

After learning to sing the first section of this song with a teacher-directed approach (until the key change at measure 42), Mr. Baker has the students turn to the inside cover of their sheet music. There, the students read the lyrics provided. Then, he distributes journals for them to write responses to these prompts:

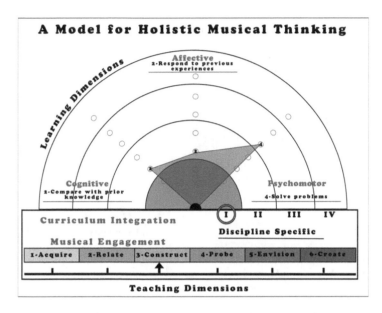

Figure 4.6 Holistic Musical Thinking Model for Vignette 2, Variation 1.

- How would you describe the mood or feeling of this song?
- How do these lyrics make you feel?
- How often do you sing when you are alone? When you are in a group?
- Does singing alone make you feel any differently when you are alone or in a group?

This activity addresses self-awareness and social awareness, two of the social and emotional learning (SEL) competencies as articulated by the Collaborative for Academic, Social, and Emotional Learning (Dusenbury et al., 2015). By asking these questions, Mr. Baker encourages reflective and inter- and intrapersonal thinking. Figure 4.7 displays the teaching and learning dimensions used in this variation.

Variation 3. In this variation, Mr. Baker uses the same teacher-directed approach to present the notes and rhythms of the song. After the singers have learned their parts for the first section of this arrangement (until the key change at measure 42), Mr. Baker has the students read the lyrics provided on the inside cover of their

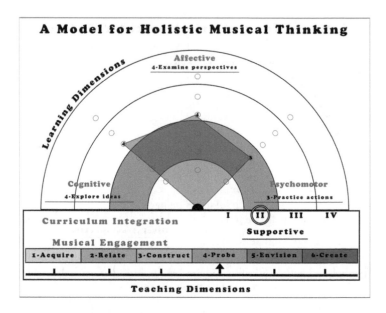

Figure 4.7 Holistic Musical Thinking Model for Vignette 2, Variation 2.

sheet music. Once they are familiar with that text, he has them listen to the professional demonstration recording provided by the publisher. The students follow along with their sheet music and listen for "meaningful moments" when changes in the music connect with the meaning of the words. During a repeated listening, Mr. Baker has the students make a small check mark in their music to indicate those "meaningful moments." With a partner, the students share their thoughts about the points of connection between the music and the lyrics. To conclude this activity, Mr. Baker gets the students' attention and invites anyone to share their observations with the rest of the choir.

To provide a more personal and meaningful understanding of the lyrics, Mr. Baker leads a discussion about being around friends versus being alone. His focus is on the social and SEL competencies of self-awareness and social awareness (Dusenbury et al., 2015). He asks the students to reflect on their circle of friends (hopefully some are in the same choir). He says, "Sometimes, we are with friends but sometimes we are alone. Because this song is about feelings of loneliness

Journal Prompts	Student Responses
I am alone when…	
I feel lonely when…	
I am alone but not lonely when…	

Figure 4.8 Middle School Choral Journal Form.

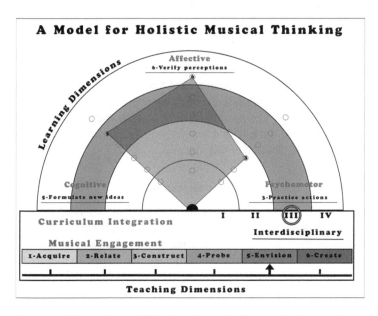

Figure 4.9 Holistic Musical Thinking Model for Vignette 2, Variation 3.

and being alone, consider if they are the same or not." He then has students journal their thoughts to complete three statements about being alone, being lonely, and being alone but not lonely, as displayed in Figure 4.8.

To conclude this activity, Mr. Baker has the choir sing through the first section of the song again, encouraging them to keep their personal journal responses in mind as they express the meaning of the lyrics. See Figure 4.9 for a display of the teaching and learning dimensions used in Variation 3.

Vignette Two Summary

In this vignette, the three variations show how Mr. Baker approaches teaching the musical content using both traditional and more exploratory techniques, e.g., rote learning of notes and rhythms, and analytical listening skills. The three variations also demonstrate how students could experience psychomotor learning in a more or less student-centered format, for example when learning the body percussion pattern. Mr. Baker's approach in variations 2 and 3 differ more noticeably in the way he expands the cognitive and affective learning dimensions. By taking time to reflect on the meaning of the lyrics and to include a journaling activity, Mr. Baker has students think reflectively. He uses the SEL competencies of self-awareness and social awareness (Dusenbury et al., 2015). He further extends their cognitive skills by challenging them to find "meaningful moments" in the music that make noticeable connections between the lyrics and the musical elements. The result is greater musical engagement, shown in the Table 4.4, along with a summary of the learning and teaching levels for each variation of this vignette.

Vignette Three: High School Instrumental Music

Variation 1. Ms. Carvallo greets her high-school jazz band for their regular morning rehearsal. The students take out their instruments and sit in their sections to warm up. For familiarity, Ms. Carvallo begins with their usual scales and articulation patterns. To prepare for their new music, *Harlem Nocturne* (Hagen / Stitzel, 1939 / 2008), she has the group play the same scalar patterns in G minor instead of B-flat major. She also uses the two-measure, syncopated rhythmic pattern from the score in measures 2–3 as a preview of this piece. See Figure 4.10 for a display of this rhythm. After some confusion and then more successful repetitions, the ensemble is warmed up and ready to begin learning their new piece.

Ms. Carvallo informs the group that they will be taking a musical journey to Harlem! To orient them to the feel or groove of this piece, she plays an excerpt from a professional demonstration recording provided by the publisher. She instructs the students to listen for the style of this music and to think of at least three ways to describe this music. After a second or third hearing of this excerpt (as needed), she invites the students to share their style descriptors with the rest of the band.

Table 4.4 Summary of Teaching and Learning Levels in Vignette 2 for Middle School Choral Music

Variation	Cognitive Processing	Affective Processing	Psychomotor Processing	Curricular Integration	Musical Engagement
1	Level 2 compare with prior knowledge	Level 2 respond to previous experiences	Level 4 solve problems	Level I Discipline Specific	Level 3 Construct
2	Level 4 explore ideas	Level 4 examine perspectives	Level 3 practice actions	Level II Supportive	Level 4 Probe
3	Level 5 formulate new ideas	Level 6 verify perceptions	Level 3 practice actions	Level III Interdisciplinary	Level 5 Envision

Harlem Nocturne

Earle Hagen
Arr. Rick Stitzel

Figure 4.10 Rhythmic Pattern "Harlem Nocturne" (Hagen / Stitzel, 1939 / 2008).

After distributing the sheet music, Ms. Carvallo first directs the students' attention to measure 2 and asks what the students notice. Some of them respond that they see the same rhythmic pattern from the warm-up exercise. She has the bari sax and the brasses rehearse that pattern from their sheet music. Once secure, she has the rhythm section join in with their parts for rhythmic security. While she teaches the opening melody to the rest of the saxophones from notation, she asks the bari sax and brass players where that same rhythm pattern returns (in measures 40 and 66). Once the melody in the saxophones is secure, she previews the return of the opening section in measures 40 and 66. The students read those sections to get a better understanding of the form of this arrangement.

Ms. Carvallo then asks students to find a place in the music where the rhythm is straight eighth-notes (i.e., not swung). After some think time and experimentation, she confirms or guides the students to find the rhythm in measures 28–29, 36–37, 54–55, and 62–63. To experience this change in rhythm, she has the students say the rhythmic counting in straight time. They then play their parts for that two-measure section. To challenge her ensemble, Ms. Carvallo asks how the students will make that transition to and from the straight time section. She has the students individually explore techniques for that transition until most are successful. To rehearse these transitions, she invites individual students to share their ideas about solving this musical challenge. Returning to the beginning of the arrangement, Ms. Carvallo ends this segment of the rehearsal by having the band play through measure 46 when the musical texture changes. See Figure 4.11 for an illustration of the teaching and learning dimensions used in this variation.

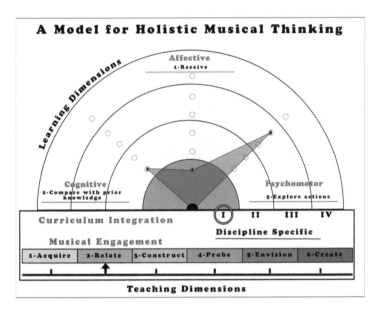

Figure 4.11 Holistic Musical Thinking Model for Vignette 3, Variation 1.

Variation 2. For the second variation of this vignette, Ms. Carvallo connects jazz with multiple art forms that flourished during the Harlem Renaissance. She describes this event during the 1920s and 1930s as a celebration of African American culture in many different formats (e.g., music, literature, and art). To experience examples of this inter-disciplinary renaissance, Ms. Carvallo has the students complete a WebQuest using *An Archive for Virtual Harlem* (Johnston, 2015). First, she displays Section 3 of this archive to orient the students to this website and to the Harlem Renaissance in general. Then, she directs students to use their own Internet-connected devices to visit the overview pages on art (Section 4) or literature and poetry (Section 20). Individually, the students read about either one of those art forms and explore some of the artists or writers profiled there. To complete this part of the WebQuest, the students work in pairs or small groups to share what they learned – both the facts and the feelings that defined the Harlem Renaissance. Ms. Carvallo instructs them to reflect about how their new knowledge could inform their performance of *Harlem*

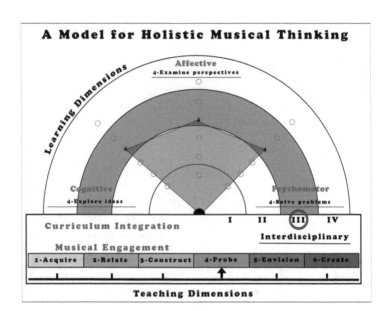

Figure 4.12 Holistic Musical Thinking Model for Vignette 3, Variation 2.

Nocturne (Hagen / Stitzel, 1939 / 2008). She asks, "How does knowing what you learned help us be better musicians?"

For the second part of the WebQuest, Ms. Carvallo presents the summary webpage for musicians in the Harlem Renaissance. She instructs the students to view three or more of the seven musicians listed there to learn more about their performances and this type of jazz music. Wearing headphones, the students individually browse the video files listed on *An Archive for Virtual Harlem* (Johnston, 2015). Then, Ms. Carvallo challenges the students to "play along" with one or more of the videos. Having to follow the recording without any sheet music or melodic reference is difficult, but most of the students succeed in at least finding the groove and parts of the melody. As they work through this assignment, many students are surprised with how well they can play along, just by relying on their musical ear. Figure 4.12 displays the teaching and learning dimensions used in this variation.

Variation 3. In the third variation of this vignette, Ms. Carvallo introduces the students to the American poet Langston Hughes

(1901–1967). She explains that he was the most influential writer of the Harlem Renaissance, a celebration of African American culture in many different formats (e.g., music, literature, and art). In addition, he wrote in a new style called "jazz poetry." This gave his poems a particularly swung rhythm or cadence and sounded like spoken improvisations. Then, Ms. Carvallo has the students read more background information about Hughes from *An Archive for Virtual Harlem* (Johnston, 2015).

After answering any questions the students have about Hughes or the Harlem Renaissance, Ms. Carvallo reads the poem "In Time of Silver Rain" while the students listen. Then, she distributes the form below and re-reads the poems. This time, she asks the students to identify words or phrases that stand out or have more significant meanings for them. Opposite each stanza on the form, she asks students to write words or phrases that capture their impressions or interpretations of that text. In other words, the students express how each part of the poem connects with them emotionally. See Figure 4.13 with the text of the poem and a form for student responses.

To translate their ideas from words to music, Ms. Carvallo has her students work in pairs or small groups. First, they share their impressions of the poem and notice how similar or different their impressions are. Then, they take turns reading either the poem or

Title	*"Lenox Avenue: Midnight"*	Student Response
Stanza 1	The rhythm of life Is a jazz rhythm, Honey. The gods are laughing at us.	
Stanza 2	The broken heart of love, The weary, weary heart of pain, -- Overtones, Undertones, To the rumble of street cars, To the swish of rain.	
Stanza 3	Lenox Avenue, Honey. Midnight, And the gods are laughing at us.	

Figure 4.13 Hughes's Poem and Response Form.
Source: Hughes (1926, p. 39).

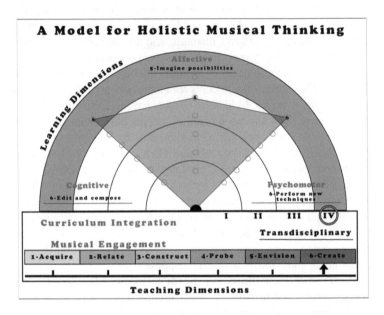

Figure 4.14 Holistic Musical Thinking Model for Vignette 3, Variation 3.

their own impressions while another student or students improvises a melody based on the words. Instead of a direct parallel, as if singing the words, the focus is on capturing the poem's emotions and the reader's impressions. Ms. Carvallo allows her students to improvise freely or to use the chord changes and meter in measures 48–55 from their arrangement of *Harlem Nocturne* (Hagen / Stitzel, 1939 / 2008). To conclude, Ms. Carvallo invites the students to share their improvisations. When complete, she also asks the class for ideas about how to incorporate those improvisations into their performance of the *Harlem Nocturne* arrangement, perhaps with a spoken section based on Hughes's poem and their responses to it. See Figure 4.14 for a display of the teaching and learning dimensions used in Variation 3.

Vignette Three Summary

In summary, notice how Ms. Carvallo focuses on performing the printed arrangement of *Harlem Nocturne* (Hagen / Stitzel, 1939 / 2008) with some intentional teaching strategies. While also devoting some attention to more general cognitive and affective learning, she

Table 4.5 Summary of Teaching and Learning Levels in Vignette 3 for High School Instrumental Music

Variation	Cognitive Processing	Affective Processing	Psychomotor Processing	Curricular Integration	Musical Engagement
1	Level 2 compare with prior knowledge	Level 1 receive	Level 5 explore actions	Level I Discipline Specific	Level 2 Relate
2	Level 4 explore ideas	Level 4 examine perspectives	Level 4 solve problems	Level III Interdisciplinary	Level 4 Probe
3	Level 6 edit and compose	Level 5 imagine possibilities	Level 6 perform new techniques	Level IV Transdisciplinary	Level 6 Create

focuses rather narrowly on the psychomotor or performance skills in the first variation. In the second variation, Ms. Carvallo de-emphasizes performing from the printed arrangement and instead spends time exploring background information about the Harlem Renaissance. She also connects that factual learning to emotional reflections and performance tasks. She expands the context for understanding, feeling, and also performing while keeping this arrangement of *Harlem Nocturne* as the basis for this variation. The third variation illustrates an enhanced interdisciplinary experience with the poetic connections to music. Using Hughes's poem "In Time of Silver Rain" as an example, they respond emotionally and musically to the text. This type of activity stretches disciplinary boundaries and challenges students to think beyond the normal expectations of an instrumental ensemble. At the same time, it offers more opportunities for musical engagement through multiple personal and curricular connections. See Table 4.5 for a summary of the learning and teaching levels for each variation.

Developing a Musical Thinking Curriculum

In this section, we look toward developing a curriculum of musical engagement. The important work of curriculum development in music education should include thoughts, ideas, and open-ended responses as well as vocabulary and activities. By augmenting students' awareness of music as a thoughtful experience, music educators can effectively engage students and encourage them to think more musically, and also inspire them to be musically independent.

This view of curriculum is at the instructional level, bridging the formal or ideal national standards and the operational or lesson plan level (Campbell & Scott-Kassner, 2019). Toward this goal, music educators can encourage and challenge students to express themselves in a number of engaging and creative classroom activities. Ultimately, the effects of such experiences will serve amateur and professional artists alike by developing enthusiastic and supportive audiences who are involved in life-long learning and continuing education.

Multiple state-wide standards emphasize thinking skills and 21st Century Skills, often including higher-order thinking strategies encompassed by critical thinking. As such, music educators cannot afford to ignore the opportunity to add critical thinking practices to their teaching repertoire. With an understanding and use of musical thinking skills outlined in this book, music teachers can increase their connectivity to school-wide and life-long learning objectives while remaining focused on teaching and learning musical content in their classrooms.

Opportunities for Musical Engagement

With respect to each of the four artistic processes in the National Core Arts Standards (2015), teachers can develop opportunities to promote musical engagement in each of the three learning

Table 4.6 Summary of the National Core Arts Processes and Standards for Music

Artistic Process	Standard	Anchor Standards
Create (Cr)	Conceive and develop new artistic ideas and work	1. Generate and conceptualize artistic ideas and work. 2. Organize and develop artistic ideas and work. 3. Refine and complete artistic work.
Perform (Pr)	Realize artistic ideas and work through interpretation and presentation	4. Select, analyze and interpret artistic work for presentation. 5. Develop and refine artistic techniques and work for presentation. 6. Convey meaning through the presentation of artistic work.
Respond (Re)	Understand and evaluate how the arts convey meaning	7. Perceive and analyze artistic work. 8. Interpret intent and meaning in artistic work. 9. Apply criteria to evaluate artistic work.
Connect (Cn)	Relate artistic ideas and work with personal meaning and external context	10. Synthesize and relate knowledge and personal experiences to make art. 11. Relate artistic ideas and works with societal, cultural and historical context to deepen understanding.

Source: National Coalition for Core Arts Standards (2015).

dimensions: cognitive, affective, and psychomotor. See Table 4.6 for those Standards and Anchor Standards.

Teachers can also promote each artistic process by designing instruction with differentiated levels of curriculum integration: discipline-specific, supportive, interdisciplinary, and transdisciplinary. In the following section, we explore each of the processes in terms of their anchor standards and possible applied teaching and learning levels.

Creating

With respect to the Creating process, when students conceive and develop new artistic ideas and work, teachers may find learning opportunities for musical engagement in the cognitive dimension by editing and formulating new ideas, such as melodic lines or rhythmic grooves. In the affective dimension, they may imagine how a familiar piece of music would sound to a novice listener or make sense of unfamiliar music on an emotional level. Creating in the psychomotor dimension could include inventing new instrumental techniques to generate sound effects or finding solutions to performance problems. More specifically, using the Anchor Standard Cr1: "Generate and conceptualize artistic ideas and work," example cognitive actions include exploring ideas for an original melody, ostinato, or rhythm pattern. In the affective dimension, students could reflect on their impressions of musical improvisations and compare those with other musical phrases. With hands-on learning activities, students could explore ways to sing or play new melodies and rhythms while simultaneously solving any technical issues. For Anchor Standard Cr2: "Organize and develop artistic ideas and work," students could edit their original musical ideas by rephrasing or revising them. Experimenting with retrograde, inversion, augmentation, and alternative timbres are all thoughtful strategies for this dimension. Affectively, students could imagine new iterations of their musical ideas with attention to the desired effect or impact. By developing musical ideas creatively, students could also consider how different parts or layers of an arrangement influence the overall musical effect. Through repeated and varied performance, students could expand their range of technical skills. For Anchor Standard Cr3: "Refine and complete artistic work," students could apply additional levels of editing to complete the composition process. Their finishing work from in the cognitive dimension matches their attention to verify their own affective perceptions of the completed work. By finalizing and setting the corresponding perform-ance techniques, students refine the hands-on or practical aspect for their finished compositions.

Performing

Realizing artistic ideas and work through interpretation and presen-tation involves the artistic process of Performing. Although students' actions in performing are largely in the psychomotor dimension, they also involve the cognitive and affective dimensions. Singing or playing an instrument obviously requires a skill set and technique practiced over time. In addition, understanding the musical elements involved in a composition is a key component of performing, as is effective and emotional interpretation of the composer's intent. In other words, technique is a requisite but insufficient stand-alone skill for musical performances. Musicians need to combine understanding and feeling with technique to translate the composer's intentions accurately and with feeling. In particular, using the Anchor Standard Pr4: "Select, ana-lyze and interpret artistic work for presentation," students demonstrate cognitive actions of choosing and thinking through musical ideas by comparison and using prior knowledge. With respect to the affective dimension, they apply their own artistic interpretations of the com-position as they make sense of the chosen compositions. Finally, they add to their understanding and interpretation of the work by singing or playing it on an instrument through practiced, repeated actions in the psychomotor dimension. For Anchor Standard Pr5: "Develop and refine artistic techniques and work for presentation," the psycho-motor dimension plays the largest role because students practice tech-nique, resolve performance challenges, and present their refined skill set in performance. Understanding the avenue toward enhanced skills (developing practice strategies) and interpreting their own emotional perceptions and reactions during the skill-building process (acknow-ledging progress and set-backs), both play important but less obvious roles in addressing this performance standard. Similarly for Anchor Standard Pr6: "Convey meaning through the presentation of artistic work," psychomotor actions play the central role, but with important contributions from the other two learning dimensions. By performing new or established techniques, students most often address this standard by translating the composer's ideas from written notation to an audible experience. Enacting the spirit and musical intention, however, requires an understanding of those ideas on a cognitive and an affective level. By involving both cognition and affect, musicians transcend the necessary technique to convey the "music between the notes."

Responding

Regarding the artistic process of Responding to works of art, the cognitive and affective dimensions play a more prominent a role than psychomotor skills. When students understand and evaluate how the arts convey meaning, they compare and contrast musical ideas while also making sense of those ideas reflectively. They assign meaning to as they interpret melodies, rhythms, harmonies, and timbres. At the same time, they relate those ideas to previous experiences and imagine new possibilities in response to their music listening experiences. In addition, students could demonstrate voluntary or involuntary movement in response to music listening. More specifically for the Anchor Standard Re7: "Perceive and analyze artistic work," one main focus is on cognitive actions. Those include analysis on the micro and macro levels, as students attending to larger and small parts of the musical form. While emphasizing an understanding of musical elements such as melody, rhythm, harmony, and timbre, this standard also focuses on perception. From an affective viewpoint, students attend to and make sense of their own musical experiences (which could be via music listening or performing). How they self-reflect on their own musical perceptions is a key part of this standard and of the responding process in general. Also for Anchor Standard Re8: "Interpret intent and meaning in artistic work," the cognitive and affective dimensions again combine as students think through or probe the composer's intention for a particular composition. They also explore contrasting ideas and perspectives on a composition in order to make sense of their performing or listening experience. With more of a focus on cognition, Anchor Standard Re9 expects students to "Apply criteria to evaluate artistic work." This involves understanding expectations and using those as standards to judge a composition or performance. While this standard may involve elements of affect to make a value judgment, the standard focuses on applying criteria evenly and fairly. Examples include evaluating how enduring or effective a particular composition is, or how successfully a musician presented a performance based on given criteria.

Connecting

The artistic process of Connecting to artistic works involves the cognitive and affective dimensions more directly than psychomotor actions. As discussed below, however, the psychomotor dimension does play a part as well. During this process, students relate artistic ideas and work with both personal meaning and external context. Understanding and analyzing the musical and non-musical content involves envisioning relationships and constructing new knowledge. To connect with personal meaning, students need to make sense of their own experiences and reflect on their own perspectives. More specifically, to address Anchor Standard Cn10, "Synthesize and relate knowledge and personal experiences to make art," students engage all three learning dimensions to combine ideas (cognitively) with a reflection on their own experiences (affectively) in order to create an artistic product (psychomotor). This combination of three learning dimensions illustrates interpersonal connections through the art form. By looking inward, students capitalize on their own understandings and experiences to envision and create new compositions. To address Anchor Standard, Cn11: "Relate artistic ideas and works with societal, cultural and historical context to deepen understanding," students focus on understanding external factors and information that shape society, culture, and history. Relating architecture or policies, for example, to the musical and lyrical elements found in popular compositions of the time connects students' understanding of both musical and extra-musical ideas.

Curricular Integration

For all four artistic processes, teachers can effectively promote musical engagement at every curriculum integration level: discipline-specific (I), supportive (II), interdisciplinary (III), or transdisciplinary (IV). With an emphasis on creating, teachers can design effective instruction that is discipline-specific (I) by focusing narrowly on musical elements (e.g., melody, harmony, form, rhythm, and timbre). At the supportive level (II), students could borrow concepts from other disciplines such as drama or English Language Arts to enhance and extend their creative work products. On the interdisciplinary level (III), teachers could make more intentional parallels between music and another subject such as mathematics by finding common vocabulary and shared ideas. Finally, at the transdisciplinary level (IV), students could re-mix ideas from music and one or more other disciplines such as dance to create a new, blended art form. By their very nature, other artistic processes are more accessible at a more narrow range of curriculum integration. Performing, for example, connects well at the discipline-specific (I) and supportive (II) integration levels. Teachers may best address learning outcomes in performance with a focus on musical elements and performance techniques, or by adding connections to other disciplines to support their presentations. Learning activities that address the responding process maybe more effective if teachers design instruction at the supportive (II) or interdisciplinary (III) curriculum levels. This type of teaching and learning expands the range of learning modalities and opportunities for students to engage (e.g., with kinesthetic, visual, and auditory experiences). Finally, given its focus on synthesizing ideas and cross-curricular understandings, connecting most naturally fits with instruction at the interdisciplinary (III) or transdisciplinary (IV) level. To address those learning goals most effectively, teachers may find natural points of intersection to allow for powerful synergy and ultimately blurring disciplinary boundaries.

Summary

Practical applications of the Model for Holistic Musical Thinking define and describe learner engagement so that teachers can foster relevant and more satisfying musical experiences for their students. The ability to enhance lessons has significance for music educators because they bear the responsibility of designing engaging and meaningful instruction for their students, with the goal of fostering musical engagement. Addressing a broad range of multi-faceted musical instruction is key to involving students; as Larson wrote, "…all these [musical] responses – aural, intellectual, emotional, imaginative, and kinesthetic – and anything else we do that gives music meaning for us" (2012, p. 31).

This Model of Holistic Musical Thinking is egalitarian. It does not discriminate based on prior musical knowledge or experience. By doing so, it honors each person's perception of music in the way that is most relevant to them. While some approaches and models of music education focus on thinking in more narrowly defined cognitive terms (Letts, 2018), a holistic approach recognizes and honors the diversity of ways that we experience music, kinesthetically and emotionally, as well as cognitively. A holistic view of music education seeks to educate through the head, hand, and heart.

In summary, as discussed in this and earlier chapters, scores of scholars and researchers have reported the value of a multi-faceted approach to teaching and learning music. By structuring interdisciplinary and experiential music education to instruct, move, and inspire learners, teachers and teacher-educators can reach more of their students and teach them on a more engaging level. By taking advantage of embodied and meaningful musical experiences, we can use this holistic approach to counteract fragmented thinking and isolated teaching. Instead, we can enhance our instruction and guide our learners to embrace the multi-disciplinary experience that is music.

Conclusion

For decades, music education in the United States has stood at a crossroads, faced with this choice: to be more inclusive and authentic, or to continue down the same traditional path. As Benedict and her colleagues wrote,

> ...the deficit model of education is often epitomized by an overly narrow definition of what counts as legitimate musical knowledge, which intimidates children who lack the appropriate cultural capital while allowing teachers to ignore much of the wealth of music that exists in the world.
>
> (2015, p. xii)

Not only has the profession wrestled with curricular content, it has also grappled with what it means to be musically inclusive, accessible, equitable, and diverse. How do we effectively challenge the *status quo?* Using the Model of Holistic Musical Thinking can open pathways toward this goal. Music teachers and teacher-educators may use this new model to address these complex issues by drawing on a broad range of teaching and learning dimensions to honor a wider spectrum of musical experiences and facilitate deeper levels of musical understanding. Progress along this direction requires musical competence (i.e., technical, relational, and conceptual knowledge) as well as understanding of pedagogical skills as defined and described by the authentic, inclusive, and transdisciplinary (AIT) framework, discussed in Chapter 1 (Johnson & Palmer, 2019; Johnson, 2020). Conceptually, an AIT approach provides an axiological lens through which music educators and teacher-educators can determine the value of pedagogical aims in order to make informed and meaningful decisions about their practice. Therefore, teachers are empowered to draw on recently established and emerging directions (e.g., culturally responsive teaching, compassionate music teaching, student-centered pedagogy, and social justice) in order to connect more readily and effectively with learners. Re-framing music teaching and learning as holistic education has the potential for greater achievement and satisfaction, in both teaching and making music.

Implications for the profession most directly influence two related areas: new settings for musical ensembles and progressive music-teacher education. In the first quarter of the 21st century, K-12 music teaching has grown to embrace a growing scope of musical possibilities. Digital technology, for example, supports the ever-expanding range of popular and commercial music available in school music programs. Teachers adopting this innovative trend seek to promote diversity, equity, and student agency by using constructivist and inclusive approach (Kladder, 2022). Modern Band (now Music Will) is one example that promotes popular music while also highlighting students' social and emotional learning (Powell, 2021). These and other examples of a more inclusive and holistic perspective on musicking re-define what it means to be a "real musician" by shifting the paradigm toward broader musical inclusivity and greater musical engagement (Johnson, 2013; Kaschub & Smith, 2014; O'Neill, 2018).

Related implications for music-teacher education have also emerged, especially since scholars have offered increasing criticism of the *status quo*. In his provocatively titled article, "Doing away with music: Reimagining a new order of music education practice," Schmidt explores ideas about reforming practices in music education and teacher-education to recognize their inherent complexity and social importance (2020). Perhaps most important to understand implications of our discussion of holistic musical thinking is the warning that Benedict and Schmidt raised when such a multifaceted topic as music pedagogy is over-simplified to a predictable and prescriptive task (2011). As Tobias wrote, "through creating virtual layers of musical engagement around musical works, pre-service music educators might develop facility and flexibly in their musical thinking and teaching" (2014, p. 224). We can reconnect these ideas to musical thinking, which directly informs music-teacher thinking, by recognizing the intellectual, feelingful, and embodied habits of mind that describe how musicians think (Don et al., 2009). Said another way, it is a misconception that music is some discrete thing "out there" waiting for us to find it. Instead, the term "music" really represents personal and meaningful experiences on multiple levels – informed by thought, emotion, and action (Cook, 2021). When we conceive of music holistically as a meaningful personal experience, we can expand and improve our own musical horizons and those for our students.

If the best ideas are not applied, they are never realized. It takes practical knowledge to create musical realities. Similarly, the most impressive compositions performed accurately without emotional meaning are mere exercises. It takes all three dimensions of learning (knowing what, why, and how) to form the whole musical experience, which is one of the most rewarding and challenging aspects of music itself. Similarly, teaching and learning music does not take place in a vacuum. To appreciate its value and possibilities, both students and teachers should explore the range of interdisciplinary and social connections.

The aim of this book is to provide pedagogical connections for music teachers, teacher-educators, and their students. As with other growing trends toward holistic education in general (Mahmoudi et al., 2012) and specifically in music education (Aróstegui et al., in press), this model takes a broad view of the music teaching and learning experience. Forward-thinking teachers and teacher-educators can thereby expand the range of their pedagogical practices by embracing the richness and diversity of Holistic Musical Thinking to enjoy hands-on and heart-felt musical engagement.

References

Aróstegui, J. L., Christophersen, C., Nichols, J., & Matsunobu, K. (Eds.) (in press). *The Sage Handbook of School Music Education.* Sage.

Benedict, C., & Schmidt, P. (2011). Politics of not knowing: The disappearing act of an education in music. *Journal of Curriculum Theorizing, 27*(3), 134–148.

Benedict, C., Schmidt, P., Spruce, G., & Woodford, P. (Eds.) (2015). *The Oxford handbook of social justice in music education.* Oxford University Press.

Brophy, T. S. (Ed.). (2019). *The Oxford handbook of assessment policy and practice in music education.* Oxford University Press.

Bruner, J. (1997). *The culture of education.* Harvard University Press.

Burrack, F., & Parkes, K. A. (Eds.). (2018). *Applying Model Cornerstone Assessments in K–12 music: A research-supported approach.* Rowman & Littlefield.

Campbell, P. S., & Scott-Kassner, C. (2019). *Music in childhood enhanced: From preschool through the elementary grades.* Cengage Learning.

Colwell, R., & Webster, P. (Eds.) (2011). *MENC Handbook of research on music learning. Vol. 1: Strategies.* Oxford University Press.

Conway, C. M. (1999). The development of teaching cases for instrumental music methods courses. *Journal of Research in Music Education, 47*(4), 343–356. doi:10.2307/3345489

Cook, N. (2021). *Music: A very short introduction* (2nd ed.). Oxford University Press.

Don, G., Garvey, C., & Sadeghpour, M. (2009). Theory and practice: Signature pedagogies in music theory and performance. In R. A. Gurung, N. L. Chick, & A. Haynie, A. (Eds.), *Exploring signature pedagogies: Approaches to teaching disciplinary habits of mind* (pp. 81–98). Stylus Publishing.

Dusenbury, L., Calin, S., Domitrovich, C., & Weissberg, R. P. (2015). What Does Evidence-Based Instruction in Social and Emotional Learning Actually Look Like in Practice? A Brief on Findings from CASEL's Program Reviews. *Collaborative for Academic, Social, and Emotional Learning.*

Emerson, R. (arranger) (2023). *Wayfaring stranger.* Hal Leonard Corporation. www.jwpepper.com/Wayfaring-Stranger/11513851.item

Hagen, E. (1939 / 2008). *Harlem nocturne.* R. Stitzel (arranger). Hal Leonard Corporation. www.jwpepper.com/Harlem-Nocturne/10052550.item

Hallmark, E. F. (2012). Challenge: The arts as collaborative inquiry. *Arts Education Policy Review, 113*(3), 93–99. https://doi.org/10.1080/10632 913.2012.687336

Hughes, L. (1926). *The weary blues.* Alfred A. Knopf, Inc.Johnson, D. C. (2020, January). *Frontiers in Authentic, Inclusive, and Transdisciplinary Music Education.* Lecture Presentation, Institute for Music Education, Ludwig Maximilian Universität, Munich, Germany.

Johnson, D. C. (2023, October). *Previewing or Reviewing Orff Schulwerk as a Creative Music Pedagogy.* North Carolina Music Teachers' Association State Conference.

Johnson, D. C., & Palmer, M. (2019, February). *Envisioning Contemporary Music Education through an Authentic, Inclusive, and Transdisciplinary Framework.* Research Presentation at the Twelfth Suncoast Music Education Research Symposium, Tampa, FL.

Johnston, J. (2015). *An archive for virtual Harlem.* https://scalar.usc.edu/works/harlem-renaissance/music-from-the-harlem-renaissance

Kaschub, M., & Smith, J. (Eds.). (2014). *Promising practices in 21st century music teacher education.* Oxford University Press.

Kladder, J. R. (Ed.). (2022). *Commercial and popular music in higher education: expanding notions of musicianship and pedagogy in contemporary education.* Taylor & Francis.

Krathwohl, D. R., Bloom, B. S., & Masia, B. B. (1973). *Taxonomy of educational objectives, the classification of educational goals.* Handbook II: Affective domain. David McKay.

Larson, S. (2012). *Musical forces: Motion, metaphor, and meaning in music.* Indiana University Press.

Letts, R. (2018). Emotion in music education. In G. E. McPherson, & G. F. Welch (Eds.), *Music and music education in people's lives: An Oxford handbook of music education, Volume 1* (pp. 285–291). Oxford University Press.

Mahmoudi, S., Jafari, E., Nasrabadi, H. A., & Liaghatdar, M. J. (2012). Holistic education: An approach for 21 century. *International Education Studies, 5*(2), 178–186.

National Coalition for Core Arts Standards. (2015). *National Core Arts Standards.* State Education Agency Directors of Arts Education.

O'Neill, S. A. (2018). Becoming a music learner: Toward a theory of transformative music engagement. In G. E. McPherson, & G. F. Welch (Eds.), *Music and music education in people's lives: An Oxford handbook of music education, Volume 1* (pp. 163–186). Oxford University Press.

Powell, B. (2021). Modern band: A review of literature. *Update: Applications of Research in Music Education, 39*(3), 39–46.

Prelutsky, J. (Ed.). (1986). *Read-aloud rhymes for the very young.* Knopf Books for Young Readers.

Schmidt, P. (2020). Doing away with music: Reimagining a new order of music education practice. *Journal of Curriculum Theorizing, 35*(3).

Tobias, E. S. (2014). 21st century musicianship through digital media and participatory culture. In M. Kaschub, & Smith, J. (Eds.), *Promising practices in 21st century music teacher education* (pp. 205–230). Oxford University Press.

Appendix

Supplemental Materials: A Model for Holistic Musical Thinking Worksheet

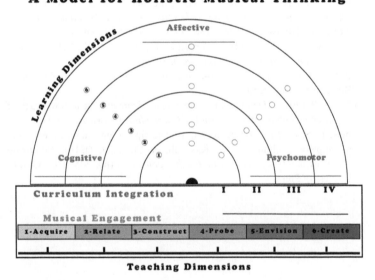

Figure A.1 Holistic Musical Thinking Model for the Appendix.

Index